First
Dollar
Feeling

Erika Heeren

DEDICATION

This book is dedicated to the American small business owner.

May these stories bring you hope
and take you back to that first dollar feeling.

CONTENTS

ACKNOWLEDGMENTS

This book would not be possible without the entrepreneurs mentioned in these pages. Thank you for your candor and for trusting me with your story.

Laura Renner
Wendy Alexandre
Michael Buzinski
Courtney Wolfe
Jeff Ehlers
Suzie Hall
Andrew Owczarek
Brandon Wright

Special thanks to the team who helped me get this project across the finish line.

Amanda Manupella, Editorial & Distribution
Anne Falk, Editorial & Distribution
Shilo Lucyk, Editorial
Dani MacGregor, Graphic Design & Cover Art

INTRODUCTION

There are a million different ways to build a successful business.

Every guru who has told you that they hold the ultimate secret formula to business success is lying. They may have found a formula that works for a selection of businesses, but the beauty of entrepreneurship lies in its fluid nature. The history of commerce is proudly annotated with people who approached the same problem differently – the great rule breakers.

It shouldn't have worked. The formula didn't make sense – *until it did.*

That's how the rock stars of the start-up world are made.

You may be reading this book feeling a little short of rock star status. You may be outright failing as a business owner. Alternatively, you may be doing well in your business, but you still doubt yourself. You may even be doing great things, but you're still not satisfied – something isn't fitting correctly. Regardless of the current state of your business and your goals, this book will help to reignite that entrepreneurial passion and guide you to the resources you need to succeed for the long haul. Before we start, there are a couple of things I need you to know.

First, I want you to know that I don't know everything about running a business. It may be counterintuitive to start a book about building a business with that information, but it's the truth. If you're struggling in business, you need that honesty more than anything. Here's another truth – there isn't an individual alive who knows everything about successfully building a business. However, there are many of us in the community who know different aspects of entrepreneurship very well. When our knowledge and experience are combined, magic happens. That concept is my inspiration behind this book.

I carefully chose nine business owners to tell their stories, including my own. I've known most of these entrepreneurs for several years. Each of these people started with the things they do exceptionally well in their businesses. Then, they leveraged those strengths and built a foundation for business success. The results are their 'rock star' moments. I knew that my experience was not enough to help every entrepreneur, but I wanted to make sure there was something in these stories for every business owner. So, just as in business - I started with the things I know very well and supplemented with the strengths of other 'rock stars' in my network. Together, our stories create a more complete picture of what it takes to be successful as an entrepreneur.

I also need you to know that, because there are a million different ways to build a successful business, sometimes our approach to entrepreneurship doesn't mesh with advice from other business owners. For that reason, it was important to me to protect the integrity of the interviews in this book. Each interview is presented in the entrepreneur's voice, telling their unique story. So, I didn't remove advice that conflicted with my own. I may not agree or approach things in the same way - so I offer alternatives in the strategy sessions you find between the interviews. What works for one business model may cause another to crumble. As you read through this book, take everything with a grain of salt – keep an open mind, try what makes sense, and adjust as needed.

Now, are you ready to get back to that first dollar feeling? Let's get started.

1 ERIKA HEEREN, THE SMALL BUSINESS MARKETING STUDIO

It would not be fair to ask the other entrepreneurs in the book to share their stories without going through the exercise myself. My entrepreneurship journey was a little more single-minded than most of the other business owners featured on these pages. I've always known what I wanted to do. I just took my time getting there. Along the way, I learned a few things about resiliency in business and breaking the mold of traditional entrepreneurial expectations.

How long have you been an entrepreneur?

I've been a 'solopreneur' for more than a decade, but I've always had a side-hustle freelance business. Those ranged from website design, reporting, copywriting, and graphic design work. I opened a full-service marketing agency in 2015 and have been going strong ever since. During this time, I've had the opportunity to work with more than 200 small businesses in varying stages of the entrepreneurial life cycle. So it's been a career full of working with Main Street business owners.

What is your business, and how did you come up with the idea?

My current business is The Small Business Marketing Studio (SBMS). SBMS grew from my boutique agency, Heeren Content & Strategy. Originally, Heeren Content was simply me and the support staff of virtual assistants and interns. As a military spouse, I was really just looking to create a sustainable job for myself. That led me to start my own business. The concept took off, and I wanted to shift my focus from merely supporting my family to creating that financial security for other military families in the same boat.

My inspiration for this business came from personal experience as a military spouse and statistical data. Military families have been struggling to make ends meet both in and after time in the service. A 2019 Military Family Advisory Network (MFAN) survey showed that 1 in 8 military families suffer from food insecurity. According to the latest Blue Star Families Military Family Lifestyle Report, more than 37% of military families reported feeling uncertain about their financial future. Overall, military families experience difficulty making ends meet at twice the rate of civilian families in the same survey. I believe this rate of economic instability could be reduced, in part, by a greater focus on sustainable military spouse employment. This concept was the catalyst for The Small Business Marketing Studio.

For military spouses, maintaining a stable civilian career while their service member is on active duty is prohibitive due to military lifestyle requirements. Military families of all core branches will move every two to three years, or around eight to twelve times during a military career. Combined with a lack of consistent, affordable childcare, this creates a situation where military spouses are statistically more likely to give up on their long-term career.

As a nation, our all-volunteer military force is only as sustainable as the family units behind the service members. When the military family cannot maintain financial security, the service member leaves the military. The long-term impact of military life on families must be considered to encourage the retention of qualified service members. This task cannot lie wholly on the shoulders of military leadership. I feel strongly that we need the help of our local business communities as well.

So, I shifted my business model from the boutique agency to a full-fledged internet company. We're essentially a subscription service for marketing support. The Small Business Marketing Studio is a marketing/public relations agency to provide military spouses, first responder spouses, and veterans with progressive careers and training in marketing and communications. My company pairs military-affiliated marketing professionals with businesses and non-profit organizations in need of marketing support. All positions are entirely remote work-based and designed to adapt to the uncertainty of the military lifestyle. At the same time, I knew that the agency needed to meet the needs of business owners as well. It had to be a win-win. So, I took my experience helping business owners grow their own companies and applied those services to my agency model.

My business model consists of four programs, each designed to empower more businesses to be veteran and military spouse friendly employers with less risk. The Virtual Marketing Professional Program pairs businesses with trained marketing professionals from the military or first responder family demographic. That professional works within the business to help them with their marketing needs. The CMO Project places experienced, executive-level military spouses and veterans in rapidly growing enterprises in need of a talented addition to their C-Suite. The Internship Program recruits military spouses and veterans who have recently left the service to gain "boots on the ground" experience in marketing while building their resumes. They work with real clients and gain on-the-job training from other veterans and military spouses with more experience in the field. Finally, a portion of all profits from my company to go toward an annual scholarship program designed to help military spouses and veterans continue their education in the marketing field.

How did you know what steps to take to make it happen?

I barely remember a time when small business wasn't a part of my life. My mother used to have a crafting business and I would go with her to the local fairs. I was responsible for signage – so, I (albeit in jest) tell people I really started in marketing at about the age of nine. I grew up in a small town in Alaska where the majority of the community was either military, employed by a small business or worked in the oil industry. I got my first "real job" in marketing at the age of eighteen, and fell in love with the industry. Now, more than sixteen years later, I have worked in different areas of communications with a small business focus. I worked full-time, and supplemented my income as a freelancer for eleven years before opening my own agency in 2015 – and I haven't looked back.

By the time I was ready to open my own business, I had over a decade of experience working with small businesses and young start-ups. So, I used that experience to find systems that worked for my own business goals. I had also been slowly working on my degree in communications and business, so I did have that exposure as well. But, I did not graduate until my second year in business – so I was really just filling in my foundation of business knowledge.

Really, what 'built' me as an entrepreneur was my time working for other businesses. One of my favorite quotes is from Vera Wang: "It's good to work for other people. I worked for others for 20 years. *They paid me to learn.*" The soft skills I developed while in college have proven to be invaluable. However, I credit my approach to business, leadership, and mentorship to the opportunities provided to me by my employers. At the same time, those opportunities are what you make of them.

Of course, as the business grew, I encountered immediate issues that were well out of my depth. So, I reached out to my peers in the local SCORE chapter for insights when I had a specific concern. That kept everything growing. I'm still young by entrepreneurial standards – so I lean heavily on the wisdom of those who have come before me. I don't forsee that changing in the future.

How did you get your first customer?

I was really tentative about venturing out on my own. My first customer as a fully-fledged business owner was actually another marketing agency. They needed support on content development, and that was my main space of expertise. I made the contact at a networking function and started picking up some of their side projects as they needed help. From there, word got around, and I had a full book of clients within ninety days. It felt terrifying. It's a big deal going from getting a client as an account executive employee - where you have a safety net of resources to being entirely responsible for the client's success. Since I was the boss, I had to be and do everything – no safety net. But, off I went anyway!

How did you get the word out about your business?

My business was mostly word of mouth for the first four years. I'd say about 85% of my revenue came from my referral partners. I never sought out a business loan or outside funding. My husband and I funded the venture ourselves, so it was essential to keep my overhead down. Building a referral network took longer, but it was also more sustainable in the beginning. Now, we've taken a percentage of our annual revenue (once we had annual revenue) for ad spend, search engine optimization, and the addition of a more robust referral building program. I also took the approach of turning all of my employees into salespeople. Each of them is empowered to sell service packages and earn commissions on closed deals. I structured my pricing so that we didn't have a cap on commissions, and it has worked well. It's also been great for fostering loyalty in even entry-level team members.

Did you encounter any roadblocks during your journey as your entrepreneur?

Several - and they are still coming. One of the most significant issues when running a service-based business like a marketing agency is that you need people to grow. People are one of the most expensive aspects of running a business. In a marketing agency, it is challenging to scale your business because you are trading hours for billables. The more you grow, the more it costs to operate - there's no room for passive income.

I chose to bootstrap my business, meaning that the business grows with profit from the business. I took on no debt or outside investors. To solve the issue of paying for people, I took a more flexible, remote work approach. Our virtual marketing assistants usually come to us as freelancers who are tired of losing their book of business when they change duty stations, or they just don't want the headache of being self-employed. All of my team members are flex W-2 employees hired near their contractor rate. They get to decide how many client hours they are available to work. Then, they only work when I have client hours to give them. Because they all have the option to sell services, they can make more money with sales commissions. Ultimately, it is more profitable for them to work for me and send prospective clients to my agency versus taking that client as a freelance client. I'm all about that win-win scenario, and I've been able to attract quality talent without drowning in payroll costs.

Another major roadblock has been military life. Currently, my husband is serving as an active duty soldier in the Army. We've been through everything from toxic military leadership affecting our home life - and therefore my business life - to a cross-country move with the business in the middle of a pandemic on a sixty-day timeframe. Even in 2020, I – like many of my counterparts – have been at the short end of staunchly rooted, backward philosophies found in the ranks of military leadership. It's one of the things that nobody likes to talk about. Life can change on a dime in the military, and you, as a spouse, are expected to adjust. No matter what you were promised, and no matter what you have going on in your own career. Military families have no recourse when the game plan suddenly changes, and all you can do is throw up your hands and say: "That's military life for you!" It's not easy to be successful in this environment. You have to be tougher than the average bear, as it were.

Unfortunately, this lifestyle means military spouse-owned businesses often have to adjust leases, employee or contractor hours, client contracts, and more. Many things go into running a business, and you are personally accountable to your clients, employees, and contractors, no matter what the military decides to do. In my case, the change has already cost me thousands of dollars to prepare my business for a major move, and I had a very short timeframe to adjust. We did it, but I can tell you that it wasn't pretty.

How did being an entrepreneur affect your personal life? What struggles did you experience? What did you learn through the process?

It's tough to be an entrepreneur. It's tough to have a successful marriage. It's tough to be a good parent. It's impossible to juggle all three and still have a social life. I believe this is the same for both men and women, but each experiences that challenge differently. It's definitely been a struggle for me.

I think the most significant impact is that I find it increasingly challenging to be in the moment. Starting, running, and growing a business requires you to keep your eye on the horizon, so you're always looking for the next step and the next progression. You're always thinking about employee growth management, financial projections, and market trends. Everything is forward.

It's tough to turn that off and live in the moment. That takes a lot of grace and understanding from your spouse, especially if that spouse doesn't have the entrepreneurial 'gene.' Your approaches to life are different - neither is wrong – they're just different. You both have to come to terms with that to reach a compromise.

For my family, counseling helped. I started my business a year after my husband and I were married, so we had the double whammy of newlywed communication growing pains and me suddenly developing the myopic obsession of building a business. Even if your marriage is solid, having an objective third party makes such a big difference when you're both trying to figure out how to make it all fit. It helps you see each other without the haze of frustration and personal triggers.

How did/do you handle negativity or naysayers?

I don't. After a while, the difference between constructive concern or criticism and toxic negativity is relatively easy to spot. I welcome constructive criticism because it helps me grow. I ignore negativity presented for the sake of negativity.

What keeps you going through the hard times?

I'm a planner. I'm really good at identifying risks and building contingency plans. That instinct has helped me a lot in business. I put a lot of time and effort into my business planning and goal setting, both when I opened my business and as it has grown. I'm always revisiting and adjusting as needed – they are both living processes. I use the LivePlan software platform because it is intuitive and keeps my financials front and center. This tool has helped me greatly as I've tried to navigate the stresses of running a business with the additional uncertainty of a military lifestyle. My business doesn't look exactly how I expected it would, but I've been able to push forward toward my goals with that plan in mind.

Looking back, is there anything that you would have done differently?

I wouldn't have held back. I doubted myself so much when I started my business. Even a couple of years in, when I was making good money and winning awards, I still didn't believe that I was "worth it." I had the trust and respect of my team, clients, former employers, and peers, but I still questioned myself. I couldn't see what everyone else saw. I still struggle with that impostor syndrome (more on that in a later chapter), but I learned to see it, identify it, and step out in faith anyway.

This doubt stems from past failures in my career, and I know many other entrepreneurs go through the same thing. When you make big moves, you tend to fail big if things go south. I have had some spectacular, expensive failures - some of which involved other people's money - making it that much worse. I got wrapped up in fear and pride, and it could have killed my business. If I could have changed anything, I would have trusted myself to follow my vision to its fullest years ago. I wouldn't have waited, and I would've gone big – no fear.

What is the one piece of advice that you would give a prospective business owner thinking about starting their own business?

Find an objective mentor, don't skip the process of writing your business plan, and leave your ego out of the equation. It is really easy to get wrapped up in the excitement of a business idea, but you need to get outside opinions to test its validity. Passion is great, but there are countless steps involved with getting that great idea off the ground and keeping it moving forward. You have to be open to taking support and advice from people who have been where you want to be.

What is the one piece of advice you'd offer to someone who is thinking about throwing in the towel?

Take a step back and ask yourself why you want to quit. I don't believe you have to keep your business going if you're miserable. Entrepreneurship is not for everyone, and it will always have its highs and lows. That being said, your discontent in your business may be solvable. You've put a lot of effort and money into your business, so you owe it to yourself to do some introspection before giving up. If revenue or cash flow is the issue – that can be fixed. If you are losing out to your competition – that can be fixed. If you feel overwhelmed and overworked – that can be fixed. If you have lost all joy in what you're doing – that may not be fixable. This is another good example of an area where a business mentor who can give you objective advice would be beneficial. If you still love what you do, take a second look at what you can change to improve your situation. It is worth it.

2 STRATEGY SESSION: GET OUT OF THE BOX

There are two hard truths you need to know about starting and running a business. The first is that there will always be struggle. Nothing about starting a business is seamless and easy. Instead, it is usually unpredictable. And, the bigger you get, the harder it is to control. This is true of every business and every industry. In the military community, we often say you've got to "embrace the suck." And it's true. You learn to love the climb, the hard times, the waiting, and the pursuit of something bigger than yourself. Positive change doesn't happen in your comfort zone, so you better be prepared to be uncomfortable. At least for a while.

The second truth is that you don't have to follow the same template as those behind and beside you. Every business is unique. The greatest entrepreneurs all have one thing in common – they found a way to do something differently. Better. More efficiently. As a small business, you have one key advantage. You're nimble. You can innovate faster, be more agile, and correct course nearly instantaneously if necessary. The big business community doesn't have that advantage.

What separates real entrepreneurs from the 'wanna-preneurs' is innovation. It's not revenue, and it's not employee count. It's making your mark on the business community by successfully bringing something different to your market. The revenue, employees, and investor capital are all by-products of that innovation.

So, before you do anything else, you need to stop and ask – "what makes me different?"

Throughout this book, you're going to hear a lot of preaching about the importance of mentors and peer connections. While these are important, you must learn to pull yourself away from the impulse to compare yourself to these other business owners and their companies. They have different inspirations, different visions, and different circumstances. You need to learn how to use your own framework to build your company.

Define What Success Looks Like for You & Your Business

It is so easy to get roped into everyone else's view of success. You think you have to hit a specific annual revenue or have a certain number of employees or clients to be considered "successful." The reality is that the only definition of success that matters when starting a business is your own.

When you get down to it, what is your goal? Are you looking to provide a sustainable income for your family? Do you want to reach $5 million in revenue in your first three years? Do you want to serve your local community, or do you want to be an internationally known brand?

Each of these goals is different, but each of them is valid. If you try to push yourself to reach a definition of success that doesn't fit your actual goal, you will lose steam fast. In fact, if you approach your business this way - you're probably not going to make it. If you do, you're not likely to find joy in your work.

For me, I got so frustrated with my career outlook as a military spouse and mom. I just really wanted to help other military spouses. So, I have had two primary goals in business. I gauge success for the agency based on how many military spouses and veterans we place in sustainable work situations. For my personal entrepreneurial goals, generating the income to fully support our family debt-free after my husband's military retirement is why I do what I do. Everything else is gravy.

I spent years fighting that gnawing feeling that I had to operate like everyone else. And I almost quit because of it. I became so burned out because I was putting in 100 hours or more a week to grow a business that wasn't feeding what *I* wanted or what my family needed. It wasn't until I was honest with myself about why I started this process that I truly came into my own as an entrepreneur.

So, I shifted the model, opened the door to new talent, and focused on my strengths. Then things started happening. Now, I have the freedom to make the necessary moves to reach my goals – and take my team with me.

There is power in that freedom.

Constructive Criticism & Haters: Learn the Difference

Your business is your baby. It is truly just as much work as having an actual baby. Trust me, I know. I have two (babies) and multiple businesses.

So, just like your baby, it makes sense that when someone tries to tell you something they don't like about your business, you may get a wee bit defensive. This feeling is normal. However, some criticism can help you grow your business more effectively. The key is learning to distinguish between which complaints are legitimate concerns and those that are just rantings from your friendly neighborhood Negative Nancy/Negative Ned.

If you have a customer leave you or a prospect turns you down, being open to the feedback can help you make your business better. You have to be receptive to hearing something negative about your business. I've learned just as much from lost deals as I have from clients who have been with me for five years.

Take the information into account, review it, and do a little research to see what happened. Then decide what you can fix for the next client or lead. If you can objectively review criticism, it's relatively easy to distinguish between a real issue and someone who wants to complain.

Remember that you're human, and you own a business operated by humans. Mistakes and missteps are bound to happen. You're going to bring on the wrong employee or the wrong client at some point in your business. You or one of your employees may not communicate effectively, and vital tasks may slip through the cracks. You may not be tracking your cash flow properly and be unable to pay your vendors for a month. These core pillars of business management take some trial and error to learn. If you're not willing to identify the holes in your foundation, eventually, it'll collapse out from under you.

Remember, constructive criticism is not a personal attack. It's an opportunity to make your business stronger.

You Don't Have to Take on Debt to Succeed

Do you know the phrase "keeping up with the Jones"? It applies to business life too. This concept hearkens back to the need to define success on your terms. If you are continually trying to reach a goal that doesn't fit your real motivation, you may be tempted to grow before you're ready. Usually, in business, that leads to cash flow issues. And cash flow issues lead to debt. Ironically, debt tends to lead to more cash flow issues because your monthly overhead goes up with every credit card swipe. It's a vicious cycle. Don't fall for it.

I struggled with this in my first couple of years in business. I knew I had a solid business plan and that the company would grow. I assumed that a significant influx of cash through a business loan would lead to exponential growth. Fortunately, I stopped and processed that concept before rushing into debt.

As I mentioned in the previous chapter, I run a service-based business – a marketing/PR agency. We grow based on the number of clients we can manage. As I bring on more clients, my overhead goes up because I have to hire more help to service each of those clients properly. So, rather than take on debt to employ several people and run a bunch of advertising to get the clients I need to pay for all of these things, I chose to grow slowly. Painfully slowly at times, but forward motion at any speed is still progress.

I'm a huge fan of Profit First by Mike Michalowicz and recommend his books to all of my clients. I moved to the Profit First model and started setting aside savings to pay for the things that would help me reach my goals. I paid for a new website, a software stack, and multiple employees from the savings of my business profits – no debt. If I did not have the money in cash, I did not make the purchase. Now, I operate with minimal overhead, I never have to sweat making payroll, and I'm even able to run a scholarship program for my employees.

When COVID hit, I had an established disaster savings fund from using the Profit First model. Like many other small businesses, we didn't see any of the PPP money or any support money at all. Like thousands of others, my business was on its own to survive. If I had taken on debt rather than adopting a lean business model, we might have had to shut our doors. Now, I know we'll recover. It's been a rough year. We've had many months where we've only broken even. But I've been able to sustain my business, take care of my employees, and not take on any debt. For me, that's a success.

My point in all of this is to encourage any fledgling entrepreneur to dare to be different. Don't fall into the trap of thinking you have run before you've learned to crawl. Grow slowly, and you'll be much more stable and have more freedom to build the life you want.

Growing Your Business Means Growing Your People

There's a lot of talk about business culture; it has almost lost its meaning through the buzzword haze. But it does matter. When you create a culture of employee growth, your people will be more invested and willing to stick around. Employees are selfish, and rightfully so. If they cannot further their career with you, they will move on. They have to think about their own goals. Entrepreneurship and employee development are two very different skill sets. You need both if your goal is to scale your business.

For my business, a culture of growth meant empowering every employee to work in different aspects of the company. I maintain an open-door policy and frequently receive training or experience requests in new marketing or sales areas from my team members. I try to facilitate these requests when possible. As the employee grows in the new skill set, they can take on more responsibility. From a managerial standpoint, that makes a "promote from within" environment easy to build naturally.

Honestly, I don't want to be always on call for my business, and most entrepreneurs dream of a life of balance and freedom that comes with being your own boss. In the early years, that's a bit of a fallacy. Right now, long hours and stress are the nature of the beast. By the time I celebrate my 10th year in business, I'd like to have a team of executives and partners who have helped me build the agency playing a much larger role in running the company. It takes work and consistent investment in each employee to create that winning team.

True entrepreneurship requires bringing something new into the market. You're a creator, an innovator, a thought leader. You don't become any of those things by constraining yourself to the same cookie-cutter template as everybody else. It's time to get out of the box and build your business on your own terms.

KEY TAKEAWAYS

KEY TAKEAWAYS

KEY TAKEAWAYS

3 LAURA RENNER, FREEDOM MAKERS

Laura Renner is a former Air Force Public Affairs Officer turned entrepreneur. Renner leveraged her public relations, foreign relations, and human resources experience to create a virtual assistant agency. Her business, Freedom Makers, connects military spouses with small business owners in need of administrative support. While Renner considers Freedom Makers her most successful venture, it was not her first. Like many veterans, it took multiple attempts to find her place in the civilian business world before getting it "right." Here is her story.

Tell me about your journey to your current business.

"When I was in the Air Force, I realized that I was interested in business. That's why, when I got out of the Air Force, I went straight to business school. I think my initial interest in business stemmed from the fact that I'm fascinated by strategy. As a business owner, you have an impact on strategy from day one. Even if you're an employee in a small company, you can still impact strategy. But in the military, you really couldn't unless you were high ranking. I didn't want to wait to get to that point.

Looking back, I see that it was a bit immature, but that's what my thought process was. So, I went straight to business school, which gave me the fifty-thousand-foot view. School doesn't provide you boots on the ground training for starting and running a business, though. Unless you're going to go the venture capital route and raise capital, it doesn't give you that type of training.

I started my first business in the 2008-2009 time frame. It was an online, dual-language children's bookstore. With the bookstore, I thought, 'Oh, I built the website, I'll just wait for them to come to me.' Of course, that didn't happen. I just sat there and waited. Then I decided to target early education teachers because the books were appropriate for children from newborn to eight years old. But our country was going into a recession then, so we didn't get a lot of traction going. I wasn't as focused on cost. I was more focused on it being a great idea, so it was something I wanted to do. Something I expected to make money from.

Of course, that never happened. I wasn't constantly trying to tinker, figure out what was working, and then improve. I didn't do any of that. I built it and was like, 'Okay, they'll come.' I went to a bunch of conferences trying to sell books, and I managed a few sales. I think it was a combination of I wasn't tinkering or improving, and the market wasn't quite there. The recession was pretty dramatic. In reality, what happened with the bookstore is I got to the point where I wasn't willing to spend any more of my cash on it. That's when my old commander called, and I was like, 'Sure, I'll come work for you.' I took the job and stayed with it long enough to rebuild my savings and pay down my credit card.

Between the bookstore and my next business, a recruiting business, I took a corporate job in HR. As I said, my old wing commander hired me, so I fell into HR. One of my successes in that company was building out their recruiting process because they didn't have an efficient one when I was hired. We were growing so fast, and we needed to be able to hire quickly. We were a thousand-person company without a system for recruiting. If we needed it, I was sure other small businesses needed it too. That's what led me to start that next business.

My second business was a standard recruiting service for small companies. I'd learned how vital innovation is between my first and second business. That realization led me to continually tinker when running the recruiting business. I was trying to build a system. I was trying to grow as a business owner, figuring out what I did and did not enjoy doing. Unfortunately, along the way, I realized that I wasn't enjoying this business at all. It was difficult. Everyone says starting a business is hard, so I thought that's why I was miserable. After a while, I realized I'm miserable because I don't enjoy recruiting.

Freedom Makers spun off of that recruiting business. Originally the recruiting business was supposed to be a consulting service where we help the businesses build their recruiting system. But my very first client was like, 'That's great, but I still need to learn to do it. Can you find me someone?' This sentiment was surprisingly common. I realized there were many business owners not ready to commit to an employee but still in need of extra help. I started thinking that maybe a virtual assistant is a service we could offer under the recruiting company.

My brother was still on active duty and getting ready to move again when I was thinking about this. I happened to be having a conversation with my sister-in-law about what she was going to do for work at their next duty station, and that's when it hit me. I was like, 'Wait a second. We could use military spouses to be the assistants because they're an untapped resource of talent.' I started talking to a few potential clients about it, and they were interested, particularly in the opportunity to give back to a military family. That kicked it off from there. I enjoyed it so much more, which is probably why it's the most successful of my businesses. Because of that, I dropped the recruiting side of the business and went straight to doing virtual assistants full time."

Tell me about your first customer. How did it make you feel the first time someone paid you for what you were selling or the services you were providing?

"I remember getting my first customer. It was exhilarating. I started my business and moved to the Bay Area at the same time. That's two major life events. Often when people start a business, they leave their job but live in the same place. They already have a network, especially if they're starting a job within the industry that they've been working. Or, if they move, they move because of a job. I moved and started a business simultaneously, which I think a lot of veterans do. You get out, move, and decide to start a business.

For me, I didn't have a network, and I didn't know anyone out here. I just wanted to live out here. So I networked like crazy. I remember when that first client said yes. I was super excited. Unfortunately, I was blaming myself for how long it took to get the first yes. But I think we beat ourselves up too much. Give yourself some slack. I think it took me three months to get my first client in the recruiting business. When it happened, I drove straight from his office to a bank, opened a bank account, and deposited his check. I probably still have that check somewhere, too."

Tell me how you got the word out about your current business, Freedom Makers.

"When I started to Freedom Makers, I had been here in the Bay Area for a couple of years. I was able to share our new service within the network I built there. I don't remember the conversation with my first client. But I remember hosting the training to train his Freedom Maker on the tasks he needed to be done. That was exciting.

For the first couple of years, new clients came from my network. With some of my networking groups, it was a five hour per week commitment, at a minimum, to be a part of that group. It occurred to me that for an attorney, consultant, or recruiter, where you only need a couple of new clients a month, that was a good investment of time. Our average client uses us for 10 hours a month, so we need a lot more than two or three new clients a month to survive. That led me to realize the networking groups were less helpful for my business.

After about a year, we switched to more of a digital marketing strategy. Interestingly, our number one source of new clients is still referrals. Focusing on providing a good service and reminding people of who we were and what we do continues to lead to more referrals. Now I'm not a part of networking groups. We post a blog every week, send out a monthly newsletter, and stuff like that.

We often get clients that say, 'I need someone to do my social media. I hate it, but I have to do it.' And I'm like, 'You don't have to do shit. You don't have to do what you don't want to do.' I notice that if they're only doing social media or digital marketing because they feel like they have to, they don't get a lot of traction with it. It's not their passion to write that blog, so they're just going through the motions.

One of my friends, a consultant, didn't have a website for her first four or five years because her business is all referrals. I mean, 100% referral based. She's a part of two or three networking groups, so she's always going out to her groups and having coffee five times a week with different people. That's how she ensures they remember her and will refer clients to her. She's on track to do half a million this year. She's doing well for a small business. She grew that without having a website until last year.

I would say you have to figure out what you enjoy. When we first switched to digital marketing, I didn't like writing. Instead, I did videos. One of my Freedom Makers would take the video and turn it into a blog. Eventually, I became more comfortable writing. Figure out what you enjoy doing, and then work your marketing strategy around that. On the other hand, some people like a challenge. I know someone else who is a consultant. She is terrified of public speaking, but she forced herself to do it as part of her marketing strategy because she wanted to get better at it. And, digital marketing doesn't make sense for every business. It certainly helps, but if you don't want to do it or don't have the resources, just focus on referrals."

Can you tell me about the major obstacles you had to overcome to find success in your business?

"I'm one of the business owners or entrepreneurs who have a new business idea every week. When I started Freedom Makers, I was like, 'If I do this, how do I know this one is going to stick? How do I know that six months from now I'm not going to be bored and want to move on to my next one?' For that reason, I sat down and thought about it. I realized that a big deal for me is freedom. That meant being able to work from anywhere in the world, at any time, and not being tied to a location. As a result, the entire model became about freedom. That principle guides everything we do.

For example, we do not have a minimum hour requirement for our clients because it's freedom for them. For the spouses, we do not assign work. They get to choose the work they want to go for, so that's freedom for them. Everything is designed to give as much freedom as possible. Sometimes people ask if we have a system that our clients must log into to communicate or work with a Freedom Maker. The answer is no. We're system agnostic. We use the client's software, so they don't have to learn something new. We just use what they use.

That became a big defining moment for the business and for me. That was part of what allowed the third business to be successful. I was focused on what I needed to get out of it to be willing to put more into it. If I didn't want to get out of bed to work on it, that's a severe problem.

More tangibly, Freedom Makers had a cash flow problem. That was a big problem for us in the beginning. We're an agency, so we pay the Freedom Makers for their work. Then the client pays us. That means there was a significant cash flow gap. Even when we were profitable on paper, we were struggling to hit payroll. What we ended up doing was asking clients to prepay. That solved the cash flow issue and, because we don't have a minimum hour requirement, allowed us to stay within the client's budget.

Budgeting client hours through the prepay system ended up being extremely helpful. Before we made that switch, there were a couple of times when the client was expecting five hours of work, and the Freedom Maker worked twenty. So, the client wasn't expecting that big of a bill. By having them prepay, we can stay within their budget, but that also solved our cash flow problem. That was a significant, more tangible, roadblock that was exciting to figure out a way around."

How did being an entrepreneur affect your personal life?

"On a personal level, I was raised to be ambitious. I felt like I needed to start a multi-million-dollar business. At the same time, I didn't want to. I wanted to have a more freeing and flexible business. We can certainly get to a multi-million-dollar business. I just didn't want that to be our sole focus and feel like we have to hustle to get there.

It's more like we're going to build it right, and we'll get there, eventually. That was a constant internal struggle. Almost an identity crisis. 'Who do I want to be, and who am I?' That struggle impacted what I was doing with the business. It compromised my self-confidence. And, of course, not having money for a while had an impact. I remember someone once said, 'The fastest way for personal growth is to start a business.'"

How do you handle negativity?

"At first, while I was going through an entrepreneur identity crisis, people would say something, and I would start to question if I was doing it right. I'd wonder if their way was better. I started to doubt myself. Over time, I became more confident and sure of myself. I realized this is how I like to do things, which is how I want it done. If you're not okay with that, we need not work together. No hard feelings. We just don't need to work together.

This philosophy applies to a lot of my vendors. I had bookkeepers questioning why I was registered in Delaware because it's an extra expense every year. I would explain that we would be a national company. If the bookkeeper was not okay with that, we didn't need to work together. No hard feelings. It's just that they didn't see my vision, and I needed to find somebody who did.

Whereas before, I was like, 'Am I wasting money? Was that a bad call? Should I give up on Delaware?' Once I stuck to my guns, it was easier to find vendors who supported that vision. But if it's an employee being a naysayer, I listen to understand their point of view. I usually try to incorporate their feedback, if possible."

What keeps you going through the hard times?

"A new morning. When you wake up, you tackle the day. When I'm starting something new, I realized that the first ten steps are lumped together as step-one in my mind. Then it gets overwhelming. We can't do it all. How can we handle all of that in one step? I'm still learning and working on breaking it down into ten steps, and then step one becomes a lot easier.

Maybe it's step five that we don't know how to do, but once we get through steps one to four, we'll have a better idea of how to handle step five. Or maybe we'll know that we actually shouldn't do step five. In my mind, all ten steps are one step, and I'm thinking about step five. So I tend to become paralyzed. I'm like, 'What if that is a mistake? It's going to kill everything.' When in reality, we'll know that by the time we get to step five.

Learning to break things down into smaller steps and focusing on the step right in front of me has helped a lot. When I catch myself jumping ahead, I remind myself to think about today. I'll ask myself, 'What are the steps you have to do today?' Then I trust that those steps will get me to the end vision. I trust that the actions I'm taking will lead to the results I want. That became a lot easier once we started getting traction and knew we were on the right path. The big lesson I've learned is just to take it day by day. Until that point, I just had to go on faith.

I also belong to a strong community of other business owners. Hearing their stories and sharing mine has been encouraging as well. A final sense of strength came from the Freedom Makers themselves. Before we got traction, I was never sure if it was going to work. I kept thinking, 'I can't quit. I can't go to them and tell them it won't work.' That clarity became encouraging after a while. I knew I couldn't let them down."

What's one piece of advice you'd give to someone looking to start their own business?

"Focus on sales. By staying focused on sales, everything else will take care of itself because it'll have to. I've known entrepreneurs who think they have to get their website, logo, and everything else set up before they can even start talking to clients. Maybe in some industries, legally, that's true. If you have to be licensed. Otherwise, focus on sales and talk to as many people as you can about what you're doing. That way you're not doing it alone. Because it can be very lonely. I have someone meet me every week. It's a standing meeting, and we talk about what we did that week. We share our successes and struggles. Then we set goals for the next week.

We do that because we started our businesses at the same time, and when you first start your business, it's a crazy roller coaster. Even once you get going, it's still a roller coaster. It's just not as extreme. By being able to say it out loud, we could see, almost outside of ourselves, what we're going through.

Sometimes it would work out that one of us was at a high point, and one of us was at a low point. The person who had a great week would encourage the person who has a bad one. Or sometimes we were both low, but we knew hearing the other person's story would help. Whenever that happened, we'd share a high five right after. Then it became a matter of inspiring each other to go farther. Having that accountability partner and being in a community of business owners has been helpful."

What advice would you give to someone who is overwhelmed or burned out in their business?

"The important thing to know is your 'why.' Maybe a client wants to hire you to work with them directly, and that doesn't align with your goals. Or you spend all the money you're willing to spend, and that's it. You're done. Those are all perfectly valid reasons to throw in the towel. The only reason I would think you should not quit is because of fear. If you're wanting to quit because you're scared, please think about that and reconsider. How can you address that fear? That's where all your growth is going to come from - by addressing that fear. You're going to have that personal growth.

I never really see things as quitting per se, but rather, you're ready for another adventure in your life. If you're burned out, bored, or want to do something different, those are all valid reasons because now you're onto the next chapter in your adventure. If you're doing it out of fear, then really, what you're doing is going back to the beginning of the book and redoing another chapter. If it's fear, figure it out, and address it. If it's not fear, kudos to you. Don't feel guilty. Just do it. Go on to your next adventure."

4 STRATEGY SESSION: FIND YOUR NICHE

What can we learn from Laura Renner's story? Like many entrepreneurs, Laura took a winding journey before finding the right business model. In fact, she had to explore multiple industries before creating the right business. If you're just starting out in business or feeling overwhelmed in your existing business – this can be a comforting concept. Even if your first business model doesn't quite pan out, that may not be the end of your entrepreneurial journey.

Small business ownership is not easy, and you have to have a passion for what you're doing to sustain it. That may be a passion for your product, for your customer, or for your mission. Regardless of where that passion is founded, if your business model does not feed that – you will burn out. You will forget your 'why' and likely eventually give up on your business. If you don't give up, you'll be working long, draining hours for something that does not feed your purpose. At that point, you're not living the freedom of entrepreneurship – you're a slave to your business.

It is a mistake to believe yourself stuck in a business model that doesn't work for you and simply throw away all your work. If you find that something doesn't fit, take a hard, objective look at what is 'off.' Then identify what is right about the business. None of that experience is a waste if you have learned from it. This may sound trite, but historically, entrepreneurs have been dramatically changing their approach to business and careers on the fly since the very beginning. It may surprise you to find that many well-known entrepreneurs took years and multiple careers or businesses to find their lightning in a bottle.

Vera Wang has been synonymous with weddings since the 1990s, and she hasn't let up since. However, she didn't start designing until she was forty years old. She was a figure skating competitor as a teen. Then she held a seventeen-year career as an editor at *Vogue* before exploring her true passion. It took her multiple attempts at success and happiness before she found her niche.

It's hard to remember a time when Amazon wasn't a household name, but Jeff Bezo's journey took quite a bit of trial and error. His career began as a product manager in the financial industry. He started Amazon (then Cadabra) exclusively as an online bookstore. Then, he had to reevaluate and expand into music and video. It was not until the launch of Amazon Web Services – a completely different platform than the original Cadabra – that Bezos realized the company as it is today. If he had stopped at books, the world would look very different.

Spanx founder Sara Blakely failed her law school entrance exams twice and was selling office supplies for seven years before creating her innovative product at the age of thirty. In 2012, she became the youngest self-made billionaire. While society likes to label entrepreneurs like Blakely as an 'overnight success,' the reality of that journey tells a very different story. It's time we honor that winding journey more than the overnight success façade.

The reality is this roller coaster ride doesn't just happen to the big-name entrepreneurs. It also happens to the mom-and-pop businesses, the 'solopreneurs,' and business owners from all walks of life. Very few 'success stories' end up on the same path they started on. In fact, as you read the rest of the interviews in the book, you'll find this theme is present in every single story. When I was selecting the entrepreneurs to interview for this book, that theme wasn't planned. It's just so statistically 'normal' that things fell that way naturally. As an entrepreneur, you are in a constant state of reinvention, and you have to be comfortable with that.

When considering reinvention as the norm, there is the fear that hopping from business model to business model will cause you to hit the reset button every time you go through a phase of change. This does not serve you as an entrepreneur. Reinvention in business means nothing if you are not building upon what you already know. None of that time in a poor business model was a waste. It was a learning experience.

If you find yourself in a poorly structured business model, don't just throw all that time and effort in the garbage. The critical component for success is that you can remove yourself from the business. It is okay in this situation to hit the "pause" button. Take a vacation (or a 'stay-cation'), do something to give your brain a break. Set a deadline for this time because you don't want a substantial amount of time to go by before you get back to your dreams. Once you've cleansed your mental palate, take an in-depth, objective look into your business. It may be helpful to engage a mentor who can provide an objective third-party view of your previous business model. Be open to constructive criticism. Identify what you disliked about your business. Then make a note of what was working in the previous model.

Armed with this information, you can build a new business model based on where you are right now and where you want to be. It can help you identify what you need to outsource, marketing tactics that just don't fit your needs, or if you're even in the right industry. Consider it market research, a litmus test if you will. If you can disseminate and apply what you've learned, as Renner did with Freedom Makers, you'll find a more sustainable growth strategy.

KEY TAKEAWAYS

KEY TAKEAWAYS

KEY TAKEAWAYS

5 WENDY ALEXANDRE, THE RESULTS BOSS & WENDY'S WISDOMS

Wendy Alexandre is a realtor, coach, podcast host, and entrepreneur who has never shied away from opportunity. While much of her career is in real estate, Alexandre's work has evolved into something much deeper. Like many entrepreneurs, her journey was one that she had not planned. Rather, it developed as she found the courage to leverage one of her greatest strengths – networking. Here is her story.

Tell me about your journey to entrepreneurship.

"Real estate was my first business. I started back in 2004, when I was 29 years old. I had just gotten a divorce and was a single mom. I had only been working part-time, but that needed to change. I needed a full-time job because I had to make ends meet. I was offered an administrative position at a real estate office. I took it and worked for about 18 months learning the back end of the business. I worked for an agent who owned a firm. That allowed me to learn accounting ledgers, all the forms, and the ins and outs of Idaho state law. I got a bird's-eye view of how things worked in the real estate industry.

One of my jobs was processing payroll for the agents, and I saw these sizeable checks they were earning. That's when I knew I wanted in on the real estate world. At the time, I was only making $12 an hour, so I got my real estate license and went out independently. That was right before the 2005-2006 housing boom, and I was pretty darn excited with my choice. I saw more money than I had ever seen in my life.

I then went to a small boutique firm called Mountain Valley Real Estate, but they went under during the downturn. Then I worked for a land developer. I bought a piece of land, and through that transaction, I went on to buy and sell more land worth millions of dollars over the next several years. Once I started doing these transactions, working with the boutique firm did not make sense anymore. My broker at the time told me he loved me and loved what I was bringing in. He felt I was making some great choices. He said he had never brokered land deals this big and thought he couldn't properly support me. He suggested that I find a larger firm that has more experience so I could continue to grow.

From there, I moved to a much larger firm, Holland. They were still a family-oriented, local, and smaller business. They then sold to Coldwell Banker. For a short time, I worked for Coldwell Banker. It just wasn't my forte. After that, I tried a couple of small firms, but none of them fit. It was right around the turn of the market in 2008 when I connected with a Keller Williams agent. We teamed up and had a wildly successful short sale business for the next four and a half years. Now I've been with Silvercreek for just over five years.

Results Boss was the next company I started. It happened organically. I was already used to teaching people using my own experience – so coaching made sense. So I jumped headfirst into an expensive coaching program and learned how to launch my own coaching business. It took off. Now my business is 100% referral based. Talking about and teaching the things I know is incredible.

My most recent venture, Wendy's Wisdoms (originally Lunchbox Wisdoms), started long before I expected it to become a business. I was in a relationship that was in a horrible place. We were trying to decide if we were going to keep trying or move in a different direction. We loved each other, but we were having a tough time trying to make things work. One day I watched this movie, it was called *The Love Dare*. It also has an accompanying book and workbook, with an entire program based on it. This whole program revolves around doing something for the other person that gives you no real benefit. But it prompts you to do something positive for them every single day. Every day I would write a note and stick it in his lunch. I was already making his lunch daily. Each little note just added positivity to his day, and that's how it started.

Soon after, I found out he posted pictures of these notes on his social media. I didn't know at first, because well, I unfollowed him because of the number of notifications I would get when he posted. Then he started sharing them on different sites and telling me about how people loved them. I was amazed. The lunchbox notes were so good for us, and clearly, it resonated with other people. So, I started making memes and feeling out how others would like it. It began to make an impact.

I attended a mastermind in January 2000 because I planned on ramping up my real estate business. I mentioned the lunchbox notes, and everyone jumped out of their chairs asking why I wasn't doing more with them. The mastermind group suggested that I create and sell memberships to this, and the ideas just kept spilling out. I was floored. The ideas spoke to my heart. These notes were something that I did because it is a feel-good thing. From there, I wondered what else I could do. I wondered if I could make some income from this and spread goodness throughout the world with it. So, it has grown from there."

What motivated you to dream past the Mastermind meeting? What inspired you to make this a reality?

"After the mastermind, I discovered my passion for travel and have been able to see and experience different parts of the world. Real estate, generally, is a very local business. I've been asked multiple times about starting a brokerage or running run my own team. But that's just not something I'm interested in doing. I've never wanted that. I want to be more mobile, which is part of why I started coaching. I saw this as another opportunity. Another leg of income that I could utilize to further the things I'm passionate about and be able to work from anywhere. So that's kind of the biggest motivation for pushing this forward.

I have a couple of things I've wanted to do for a long time. One of those things is to interview other people. I've been blessed to know some incredible people. I've been able to pull from their knowledge and experience and learn from them. Now I want to share all of that goodness with others. So that's kind of the next big thing for Wendy's Wisdoms. I've started tapping into those people and that knowledge, and I plan to create something else to share in a more visual format. I love technology, so sharing on video and podcasts is exciting! I want to take advantage of the technology that's available to us and share even more."

Tell me about your first customer.

"I think the one that was most impactful for me was my first customer in real estate. I had only had my license for two days before I secured my first client. They came into an open house I was doing. Everyone warned me that I'd never find a buyer there. Well, this being my very first experience, it was all super exciting for me. The clients had no idea how new I was, and I was just in my twenties. But, they trusted me. It was amazing. We looked visited at least 50 homes over the next several months.

Then we found their home. They were an older couple; he was a pilot and had so many stories to share. It spoke to my heart. We ended up building quite a relationship, and still, to this day, 15 years later, they continue to invite me to their holiday get-togethers. We even exchange phone calls.

They showed me that this business was so much more than making a sale. I thought I would have to lean on sales skills and things like that to be successful. If I never recognized that assumption to be false, I think my business would look completely different than it does now. But I am creating relationships while in this business. It has not only made my real estate business successful but allowed me to move into the coaching space so quickly. The relationships were already there, and the referrals came from that."

How did you get the word out about your business?

"I'm sure people have heard this before. But in any business, your number one priority is to market your business. I don't care what your business is. If it means you're marketing yourself as a person or marketing your product or service, 80% of everything you do as an entrepreneur is marketing. The other 20% is doing the paperwork and the things that are your business. But first and foremost, you have got to be a marketer.

I've tried marketing in multiple ways, but my most successful method has been social media. For me, it's been a matter of adding value for the people who read my content. I look for ways to provide information that will inspire them to do something different. Any marketing I do, it's always been to create value for the other person.

Will I get something back in return? Maybe. There's not a definite return on investment, though. I don't sit and think I'm going to get three referrals for every post. It just doesn't work that way. It goes back to relationship building. I am adding value to create a relationship so that I'm the person they refer to when needing what I offer. That's the way it is in any business. You have to create that relationship.

I also do a lot of other different things, like hand-deliver little personal gifts. I go to networking events on occasion. I send postcards to some people. It just depends on the person. It depends on the purpose of the marketing, but it's always based on the desire to add value first and foremost. So that relationship is still what drives their referrals. I want them to think of me for real estate, coaching, and inspiration. I want people to go and look for those 'lunchbox wisdoms' regularly because it changes them. It affects how they think and how they operate in their world."

How has your educational background influenced your decision to become a business owner? Have you used other resources like coaches and mentors? Do you believe it has contributed to your success?

"First of all, I firmly believe in coaches. Not only for helping guide you down your specific pathway, but also for helping you manage the nitty-gritty on a day-to-day basis. It just helps to have someone to hold you accountable. Someone you can bounce ideas off of. I have had multiple coaches throughout this whole entrepreneurial journey. Sometimes they were specific real estate coaches and other times general business coaches.

Sometimes my coaching has been in more of a mastermind like setting, in a group with multiple like-minded people. A group like that helps hold you accountable. Being in a group provides an environment to ask questions about anything that may pertain to growing your business or yourself. There are platforms online you can use to help educate yourself and improve as an entrepreneur. I don't think you can make this journey alone. Having that community is invaluable. There are also software and sites online that can teach you things you've always wanted to know. I think they're valuable too.

I learned graphic design in college. It was fascinating. But at that time, you needed to be in New York or California to secure a job in that field. I will tell you I'm so incredibly glad to have that education. Knowing how to do all of that and have a creative eye has allowed me to make my marketing materials. That led me to help other agents and professionals in different fields who couldn't afford to pay someone for marketing. It was great being able to teach them how to do those things."

Would you say you've encountered any roadblocks along your journey as an entrepreneur? If so, how did you overcome them?

"There have been so many roadblocks along the way. In any entrepreneurial journey, there is no way you can move forward and become better at what you do without having those roadblocks. If it were easy, anyone would do it.

The biggest hurdle in any entrepreneurial journey, especially in mine, has been learning how to handle my finances. Being an entrepreneur doesn't come with steady paychecks. No one is going to make my car payment for me. In the beginning, it was so easy. The real estate market was at an all-time high, and I made a lot of money. But I learned many hard lessons over the next six years on how to manage that money. You have to be careful not to spend all that money because it's easy to spend. That was probably the most important and hardest lesson or roadblock that I had to overcome.

It would have been so easy for me to leave the real estate industry at that point and just go back to a regular job. It would have been so much easier, honestly. But I knew it wasn't the life for me. I couldn't go back to a life of not having the freedom to attend my kid's games or help in their classrooms. I loved being available to go to lunch at a moment's notice. So I struggled and made it work."

Let's talk a little bit about that family/work balance you mentioned. Tell me a little bit about how being an entrepreneur affected your personal life. Did you experience any struggles trying to find that work-life balance? And what did you learn through that process?

"To be completely honest. I don't believe work-life balance exists in real life. I think you make time for whatever you feel your priorities are. It's all a choice. We all have the same amount of time every day, and whatever you choose as a priority is what will be a priority. If you feel that spending four hours every day dedicated to your family in the evenings is your priority, then absolutely - that should be your priority. If your preference is to make a million dollars, then that's your priority. There's nothing that says what's wrong or right.

Most of my clients work from eight to five, which was also when my kids were in school. So that's when I could volunteer. I knew that my clients were going to need me in the evenings. As a coach, it was the opposite. I find most of my clients want to work on their business during the day. Some prefer to talk first thing in the morning for accountability. That allows me to still work in my real estate career and do things in the evenings and on the weekends.

It has nothing to do with what the world would say is work-life balance. I have the balance in my life that I chose to have, regardless of what those things look like. But I've been accused of being a workaholic more than once. So, I don't know that my balance necessarily the same as someone else's."

What keeps you going through the hard times?

"Oh, routine. Honestly, it's a routine. There are some days I have gotten out of bed and cried as I drove myself to the gym. I've also sat at my desk, struggling to finish something because I was too tired, sad, or frustrated. Those negative feelings are going to happen. No matter what. The difference for me is that I have set up regular routines stick to on a day-to-day basis. If I can get that forward momentum going, it moves things along at a much better pace. I feel like if I had to decide what I was going to do based on the type of day I'm having, my day would never happen.

I have had those days where you get out of bed and have no clear direction. So you find yourself walking around in your slippers and robe with a cup of coffee, and three hours later, you realize you've been surfing social media the whole time. And nothing has been accomplished. You have to live your life by design, not by happenstance."

What's the one piece of advice you would give to somebody who's thinking about starting their own business?

"If you're doing it for money, you're doing it for the wrong reason. If you're doing it for fame, you're doing it for the wrong reason. If you are doing it because you love doing it, then that's the only right reason to go into business. You have to love the journey. You have to learn to love the grind. You have to learn to love the daily monotony of it so much that it will push you through everything else.

Because some days are incredibly hard, and some days are pure joy. There's no doubt about it. Sometimes I love every bit of it, and I'm so excited. I'm jazzed. Those are great days. But the humdrum of what has to be done every single day by far surpasses the time that you'll spend enjoying it. And if you don't want to embrace the possibility of failure and the risks involved, don't even start."

What about somebody who has been in their business for a while that might be stuck and overwhelmed? Maybe things aren't going well for them, and they are thinking about giving up on their business. What would you say to that person?

"I think they'd need to take a step back and look at what brought them into that business in the first place. What was it they originally loved about it? Where has their business taken them so that they no longer love it? How can they restructure their team or hire someone to take over the business pieces that are dragging them down? Then allow that additional help to come in so they can get back to the part of the business they originally loved.

These feelings will happen a lot throughout the entrepreneurial journey. But you have to look at it as an opportunity to say to yourself, 'Okay. I'm not learning anymore, and I'm not challenged. I'm not excited. What can I do to take a step back?' Then look at how you can leverage the resources you have. Ask yourself how you can restructure the business so you can do all the things that you loved to do."

6 STRATEGY SESSION: THE SIX RELATIONSHIPS YOU NEED IN BUSINESS

A basic Google search for Wendy's business presence shows one clear theme: people. As simple as that sounds, Wendy is known for the great care she takes in growing her network. She puts a great deal of effort into supporting other entrepreneurs, and you're hard-pressed in the local community to find someone who has not at least heard of her. This presence took years for her to create, and she has been diligent in nurturing the relationships that brought her to where she is today. No matter how big digital marketing becomes, the core of business success still lies in the opportunities you build with other people.

When you start a business, it is tempting to focus on one thing: getting new customers. Don't get me wrong, as Laura Renner mentioned in an earlier interview, sales is obviously vital to your success. However, an issue arises when you become myopic in that endeavor. In the pursuit of just getting the sale, you may find yourself casting aside other relationships vital to your business's sustainability. In your – albeit understandable – desire to make immediate money in this venture you've started, you're set on one thing: what you can get out of that relationship. While you may get new customers, the cost of this approach is high, especially as you try to grow your business in the long term.

Just like in life, there are certain relationships you want to build with intention in your professional world. Whether you are just starting in business or working with an established brand, you'll want to start by taking inventory of your existing relationships. Then, you'll need to identify what you can bring to the table in each situation. If your answer is your product or service, it's time to go back to the drawing board. Let's break down the key relationships you need in business, and then we'll delve into the best approach to creating a win-win for you and your network.

Relationship #1: Your New Customer

I know I led this chapter with a warning against focusing solely on creating new customer relationships, but that doesn't mean that these relationships aren't important. They are essential – pivotal, in fact. You cannot keep your business open without them. It is also important to remember that they are not the only relationship you should focus on, nor should that relationship be a short-term endeavor.

In the past few chapters, and in the chapters to follow, there are various strategies for getting those new customers. What you don't necessarily see in the interviews is the amount of time and testing it took those business owners to get a consistent flow of new customers coming through the door (or the website). In reality, that one to two sentence summation of those marketing strategies really took six months to a year, and up to tens of thousands of dollars, to figure out.

Generally, when launching a new marketing and advertising plan designed to bring in revenue, experts usually advise a budget of seven to ten percent of your revenue. The actual amount depends on how quickly you want to grow. If you have a desire to scale very quickly, a marketer may recommend a budget higher than that ten percent. So let's take a minute and look at that concept through the lens of small business sustainability. According to this time-tested philosophy, if you are the average American employer business making less than $390,000 per year in revenue (Census.gov, 2019), you should be spending just over $27,000 in marketing and advertising every year for marginal growth. For a more robust growth rate, you should be spending between $36,000 and $39,000 per year. The higher your revenue, the higher your marketing spend, within the same percentage range based on your goals. The majority of that money typically goes to the end goal of bringing in those new customers.

That's just the recommended monetary spend. There is also the time spend to think about when building your new customer relationships. If you have been in business for less than five years, you are faced with the burden of building trust because you do not have an established brand. If your business has been in the community for a considerable amount of time, you are more likely to be able to lean on existing brand awareness when considering your sales closing rate. Either way, you will need to be constantly selling, constantly pitching, and constantly cycling through a revolving door of customers if you only focus those efforts on new clientele. You can outsource your marketing and advertising efforts, but you will still have to be hands-on regularly to be successful. This is your business, your brand. You cannot be a bystander in your own vision.

Chances are, by the time you get a first-time customer, you are already either breaking even or in a cash deficit, margin-wise. That's normal and part of the process. Many businesses fail because they only focus on that first-time customer relationship and get lost in the cycle of constant pitching. So, you never actually make any real money on that customer until you get to the second stage of that relationship. This brings me to the second relationship you need for your business to be successful.

Relationship #2: Your Existing Customer

We've established that new customer relationships are important, but mainly because they become existing customer relationships. According to the Harvard Business Review, acquiring a new customer can cost between five and twenty percent more than retaining an existing customer (Gallo, 2014). Ideally, these existing customers become loyal fans of your business and share that love with their own network. That's when you start cooking in the revenue department.

If you build these relationships correctly, you'll need to spend fewer promotional dollars getting the word out about your brand, simply because the people who have already purchased from you will be out there sending you a steady stream of new business. Remember all of that time, effort, and money I mentioned before? If you don't have that kind of revenue to spend on marketing – or even if you do – a referral-based business will get you more significant results for a fraction of the cost.

So, how do you make your existing customers fall in love with your brand? I like to use the analogy of marriage when coaching clients on customer relationships. When you first start out, everything is lollipops and roses. It's exciting, fresh, and new – just like that newly signed contract or new purchase. Shortly after that, while you still (hopefully) like the other party, it takes work to keep that spark alive. You wouldn't go months without talking to your spouse, so why on earth would you allow months to go by without connecting with your existing customer base? They are the foundation of your business revenue. Without them, your company will fail. It will not be sustainable.

There are a few simple strategies that any business can use to maximize their customer base. The first - and easiest - is to establish a monthly email newsletter. While this is the low-hanging fruit of customer engagement, if you are a new business or have been remiss in staying connected to your customers, it's a good place to reintroduce yourself. Keep the copy simple but useful. Do not use these newsletters to pitch your services, but rather to provide immediate value to your audience. For example, a boutique retail store may include a local events list for its audience. A home-services business may include a checklist of ways to winterize your home. An accountant may pen an article on how to file your receipts for tax season properly. Don't pitch – but remind your audience that you are there, and you're an expert. You can always include a section of things that are happening in your business – new hires, discounts, events, and the like – but don't make it the focus. The goal here is to begin to build a relationship where you send that customer information, and they take the time to open and read it.

Another simple thing you can do to engage your existing customer base is to create a loyalty program. This will look different for various industries, but I've found there's usually a way to make it work for most businesses. Basically, a loyalty program provides an incentive for your customers to continue to work with your business. The coffee shop punch card is a good example. An HVAC company may offer certain discounts to customers who sign up for annual service. An online store may offer a special birthday discount or other exclusive deals for those who sign up for their email distribution list.

One key piece of advice I give to my clients regarding their existing customer base is to avoid the trap of only providing new customer discounts. New customer discounts are useful for bringing in first-time clientele, but they may perturb your existing customers who just paid full price for the same thing. But if you have a loyalty program as an alternative for your current customers, that appropriately distributes your discounts while increasing sales overall.

Your existing customer base – whether they had a positive experience with you or not – is your greatest source of data to make your marketing efforts as effective as possible. Businesses pay market research firms north of $25,000 for this type of data, but you have it sitting in your sales records. It's time to dust off that list and make the most of that investment. Send out once or twice a year surveys to engage your customers. The data you collect from these surveys can tell you what is working about your product or service, what's falling short, and which marketing avenues are actually converting sales. Most importantly – here's the million-dollar idea – address any concerns or product issues promptly.

Finally, the best way to foster loyalty with your customers is to treat them well. This seems relatively straightforward, but the practice is often overlooked. Not every customer will be the right fit for your business, but you must show respect for each and every person who makes a purchase from your company. If a customer is unhappy, fix it. If the customer is unhappy, and the issue is not your doing, find a way to diffuse the issue professionally. Hold your customer-facing employees to a high and consistent standard of quality care, and empower them to handle any issues that arise. There will always be customers who simply want to complain or game the system, but the majority of people who buy from you will tell a friend if they are treated well when things go wrong.

Relationship #3: Your Referral Partners

Just like your existing loyal customers, building relationships with complementary businesses can help you scale your business faster and at a lower cost. Unlike customers, you don't have to spend initial marketing dollars to get these referral partners. When I launched the first iteration of the agency as a solo venture, I started networking with intention. I sought out business owners and professionals who worked with the same clientele, and I took the time to get to know them. I frequently attended local chamber events, BNI groups, and other local networking groups. Not every professional was the right fit, but I soon found a group of like-minded people who held a high standard and resonated with my approach to client care.

The only marketing budget I had was the fees to attend the networking events, yet I hit my one-year revenue goal in ninety days using this method. Years later, even after I adapted my business model, those original referral partners still send me business. How? Time, effort, consistency, and clearly identifying my ideal referral partners were early on in my business. I actually have profiles of optimal referral partners written in my business plans. For service-based businesses, a solid referral network is invaluable.

First, let's identify the difference between a networking contact and a referral partner. Networking contacts are more surface-level relationships. They are great for making connections, maybe getting a few clients, and general brand awareness. In a referral partner relationship, you know the ins and outs of each other's business. You know each other's differentiators and ideal clientele. You send business back and forth and may even work together on a joint venture. Referral partners are the cheerleaders for your business.

How can you build these referral relationships? Networking is a great place to start, but you cannot be passive when building referral partnerships. If you meet someone you resonate with, invite them for a one-to-one conversation and grow the relationship from there. I like to break up those initial meetings into two discussions - one appointment where you learn all about their business, and another where they learn all about yours. If everything still feels warm and fuzzy after those initial meetings, do a little research.

A good referral partner is someone you can send business to as well, so you're putting your credibility on the line by embarking on that relationship. Just like you would run a background check on a new employee, look into the background and reputation of your prospective referral partner. In some cases, it may be appropriate to try their product or service yourself. Take special note of their online reviews because you need to know what their clients have to say. Ask your other referral partners if they've ever worked with your new contact. Essentially, check their references before moving forward.

Once you feel comfortable with your new referral partner, continue to stay in touch with them. Check in regularly and ask if there is any specific type of client they are looking for at the moment. This should be a two-way street. If you expect them to send you referrals, you need to be sending them business as well. After all, if you have a referral to share but two competitive referral partners, chances are, the one who has sent you clients most recently is going to get that referral. Be an engaged referral partner, and you'll find the relationship more rewarding in the long run.

If you want to take this a step further, some service-based businesses create referral partner programs that provide profit share on closed client accounts. Essentially, when someone refers business to you, you may send them a check for 5% of your profits for the referral, like a sales commission. This does not work in every business or industry due to regulatory issues. The financial industry is an example of one that prohibits this type of referral incentive. But if it is appropriate within your industry, a program like this serves as an added incentive for your referral partners to send business to you.

Remember, quality leads are gold to a service business. Multiple businesses are competing for your clients. Similarly, numerous people are competing for the best referral partners. You have to bring something different to the table to be competitive. Incentive-based partner programs are an effective way to set yourself apart from the crowd.

Relationship #4: Your Industry Peers

Connecting with your industry peers (and possible competitors) may seem counterintuitive. In an already competitive economy, why would you want to build relationships with other businesses in your industry? Isn't that like supporting the competition? Not necessarily. This is where putting a more altruistic mindset to your business practice can pay off.

Some of my most effective referral partners are industry peers. Many of them perform the same services I do but specialize in a different niche. These referral opportunities manifest in a variety of ways. Sometimes, we support each other when one company has overflow and needs a few extra hands on deck. I have white-labeled multiple projects for bigger agencies throughout my career because the revenue supports my business, even if I don't get all the credit. Also, when I need a supporting service, I have a solid foundation of trust built with other talented professionals. This means a quality product is delivered to the client, which makes my business look good. These relationships don't form overnight, but they can help you manage economic ebb and flow.

If 2020 has taught us anything as business owners, it's that nothing is certain. Things can change instantly, without warning. When this happens, having a trusted person in your industry who knows your market can be helpful in navigating the troubled waters of an economic downturn. Compared to Corporate America, small business owners are fortunate in that we can adapt our businesses faster and with greater innovation. That competitor down the road may turn into a partner in a time of crisis. You never know.

However, the only way to create that atmosphere of collaboration over competition is to start early – not when you need it. This is business, after all, one of the most cutthroat facets of life. If you haven't built trust with your peers, they likely won't be there when something catastrophic happens.

Anytime I coach a new entrepreneur, I always recommend that they connect with their industry association. It's the easiest way to connect with your peers. Industry affiliations bolster credibility, provide valuable market research for your industry, and can open the door to potential partnerships. A simple Google search of your industry and the term "trade association" will provide you with options to engage. Start there and build.

Relationship #5: Your Local Media

I am going to share a dirty little secret from the public relations industry. You do not need a high-end PR representative to get your business in the media. You do need an active relationship with the right members of your local news publications, television stations, radio stations, and podcast hosts. If you're not a great networker, this is where having a communications professional can help you reach those connections and get the word out about your business with some free press. These professionals have a substantial rolodex and existing relationships with reporters. In some cases, reporters may even reach out to trusted PR reps to see if they represent someone who would be an engaging interview for a story the reporter is building. There is value in that, but you can also create that network yourself.

Ideally, the best way to engage members of the media is to meet with them one-on-one, but that's not always feasible. The key to building a good relationship with your local media is to understand what the reporter or media outlet needs from you. Journalists do not care about your sales pitch. They care about the valuable information you can provide to their readers or viewers. Start by reading or watching stories from reporters who cover the type of content that aligns with your business. Then, send them stories that fit within the current news cycle. Use data, visuals, and engaging storytelling to show why your message is essential for their audience. Make it easy for them to use what you share, and be available for their follow up questions and requests. Never send your story ideas on a Monday or Friday, and always follow up within three business days. If your story does not get picked up, start at step one, and try again. You'll need to find that sweet spot of being featured as an expert in your business without pitching your business.

If you're feeling shaky about this process, sometimes it helps to partner with a non-profit organization. Often, press releases from non-profits are picked up by journalists because they directly tie to a need in the community. So, you can sponsor an event or a food drive to get your business name in the media. It also provides you an opportunity to engage with individual reporters who may be more likely to read your story pitches down the road.

Relationship #6: Your Community

Expanding on the non-profit partnership concept, I cannot emphasize enough the value of cause marketing for small businesses. Statistics show that American consumers prefer brands that hold socially conscious business models (SAP, 2018). Sponsoring a non-profit event, like a food drive or a clothing drive, can help expose your brand to a wider audience. You'll want to find non-profits that fit with your company mission. Then introduce yourself and discuss creative ways that your business can support that organization. The more visible you can be in your community by giving back, the more likely that community will engage with your business.

KEY TAKEAWAYS

KEY TAKEAWAYS

KEY TAKEAWAYS

7 MICHAEL BUZINSKI, BUZZWORTHY INTEGRATED MARKETING & BETTER THAN HOSTING

Michael "Buzz" Buzinski is an Air Force veteran turned entrepreneur. Or, perhaps it's the other way around and then back again. Either way, Buzz has built a reputation for innovative marketing solutions for small businesses in Alaska and beyond for more than fifteen years. Since marketing is such a key pillar of business success, I hope that another agency owner will better help you, the reader, discover new and creative ways to grow your business. This is Buzz's story.

I know you've been involved in several different ventures – how long have you been an entrepreneur?

"I've been an entrepreneur since I was 15 or 16 years old. My first business was a photography business - Eagle Eye Photography. I did outdoor portraiture. Instead of senior studio portraits, I would take people up into the mountains to get amazing backgrounds and natural backdrops. The backcountry near where I lived at the time, in East Bay San Francisco, was the backdrop for my photographs. That was my first business. But, the current business I have now has been around since 1999. So, about twenty years."

Tell me about when you got your first customer. The first time somebody bought into your idea, paid money, and trusted you?

"I got my first customer as an entrepreneur when I was a hobbyist photographer. I remember my first client ended up being a girlfriend. Her younger sister needed her portraits done. When I did that, and it all went as planned - I remember feeling empowered. That entire process of delivering the photography, as far as the photoshoot and being in charge of everything, was just so nerve-racking. You're the only one to turn to, and half the time, you're making it up as you go - especially when you're that young. When I got done, I sent them an invoice, and I got a check for it. That was exciting. That was the most liberating and self-gratifying action that I'd had up to that point."

Focusing on Buzzbizz – your longest-running business - and all of the iterations that have come out of it, what motivated you to take that dream and make it a reality?

"Before starting Buzzbizz, I was in the Air Force for ten years and had been playing semi-professionally as a musician. When I got stationed in Alaska, I quit being in bands and switched to more songwriting, recording my own stuff, and building out my studio. In 1992, I built my first home studio. It was a little four-track cassette and multitrack recorder. I still have a picture of me playing around on that. I made up these small shelves between my closet and my bathroom, and those two rooms were my sound rooms.

Buzzbizz Studios was originally a recording studio built to serve the working musician. I was a working musician for about 15 years. A working musician [for reference] usually has a full-time job but gets paid to perform on the side. Working musicians are usually building towards a full-time profession in music, either in performing music, writing music, or recording music.

When I originally built Buzzbizz Studios, it was to allow working musicians to have a good, productive experience in the studio. It gave them a product that they could then use to progress their career with. Unfortunately, basing your survival off of starving musicians is a horrible business plan. Within the first year, I began to use my other talents in graphic design. Over the years, it evolved from a recording studio to a production studio, and then to a marketing agency and creative agency. Now it's been dismantled so each of those pieces can work in their own and grow in their own direction, while still feeding the needs of each of the other divisions."

How long did it take in your business before you were able to pay yourself?

"I had to pay myself immediately. When I got out of the Air Force, my last paycheck was on July 15th, and the rent was due on August 1st. That was in 2005. I managed to get my cost of living down to $500 a month with all utilities paid. I actually paid two and a half times as much for the rent for my office as I did for where I lived. In total, I lived off of $24,000 the first year I was in business, which was a third of what I brought in revenue-wise."

You didn't retire from the military, so you didn't have a military retirement, correct?

"I had zero money. I just got a divorce and sold my house. We made a bunch of money off of the house, which we then split. But I used the $22,000 I had to build out my studio. I had no money in reserves either. I jumped off of a cliff into entrepreneurship. It was do or die, literally. I don't suggest that to anybody. In my defense, I did work for three years on the side in the industry I was getting into. I did a lot of networking. I gave up a lot, probably even gave up my marriage at that time to pursue my dreams. The money that I was making on the side was financing for probably 60% of what I needed to start my business. That last $22,000 was for the build-out to have a professional place to base my business. I would never tell somebody to go from zero, having nothing set up, to doing business and thinking that within the first month, they're going to figure it out.

There was a homeless guy I 'adopted' who helped me. He kind of recruited himself. On day, he saw me and noticed I did a horrible job painting the walls, so he offered to paint them for me. The price was right, so I hired him. Then, I needed carpet but didn't have the money to pay someone to help. So, he and I figured out how to lay carpet. I needed help, and he needed a place to stay. I didn't have an alarm system. But I had a couch that he could crash on, so he became my alarm system. Then, during the day, he started making cold calls out of the phone book to sell business cards to people. You just find ways to make money so you can get to the next month, next quarter, or next year. If you're in survival mode, you do what needs to be done and take advantage of every asset that you can come across to make it happen."

Which would you say is your favorite business?

"My favorite is my newest venture, which is Buzzworthy Integrated Marketing. Its spinoff is going to be Better Than Hosting, and I'm launching it next month. That's because the business plays to my strengths and love of art, digital, and working with business owners."

Tell me about that one.

"Buzzworthy Integrated Marketing focuses exclusively on web

development and integrated marketing using the website as the central point of communication for inbound marketing. We utilize mass media, traditional media, and digital marketing tools to accurately track progress and measure return on investment (ROI) down to the penny. I can tell people why they're either succeeding or not. This level of data-driven insight holds a significant amount of integrity. It creates deeper relationships between my clients and me.

Back in the day, when we did TV, radio, and print, it was tough to track ROI unless you had a coupon or special phone number. In this day and age, you can dashboard any metric and key performance indicators (KPI) you want. It just makes my job that much easier to get people pointed in the right direction because I can show them what works, taking the guesswork out of the equation. I can also show them what's available or possible, which allows my entrepreneurs a lot of freedom in making their decisions. It creates a lot of power for them because they can make informed decisions on whether they want to move forward, sideways, or backward.

Then, I created Better Than Hosting - which is splitting off of Buzzworthy Integrated Media because it played more in with the web development side of the business. This is a WordPress security platform that has a hack-free guarantee. We're going to be the only company that has this. There are 380 million websites that get hacked every day, and 90% of all web sites that get hacked are WordPress websites. For small business owners, that sucks. When your website goes down, it's terrifying.

I wanted to create a completely automated product that gave users security. If anything were to happen, they know somebody is watching and making sure it gets back up quickly. They don't have to spend hundreds of dollars paying a technician to un-hack it, get it fixed, and then deal with all the repercussions of it being hacked. We're so confident in our product that we're giving a hack-free guarantee, and the only thing that users pay is $50 a month. They never have to worry about updates, security protocols, or anything like that. We take care of it all. So that's an enjoyable project that's going to be coming out of what Buzzworthy. It's been incubating for a while. It was part of our process to make sure that websites stayed up and functioning. It's fun to watch stuff grow out of what other things you're doing."

The Better Than Hosting is more of a subscription-based model, then?

"Yeah, Better Than Hosting is a full-on subscription model - which is very popular nowadays. It's an automated process where people just set it and forget it. They get a report every month on what's happening with their website. They get a cool, super simple report that tells them their site speed, overall health, and updates made in the month. All that good stuff."

With Buzzworthy Integrated Marketing, are you doing away with the Buzzbizz Studios as it is and moving the agency to that, or are you still operating the agency model in addition to Buzzworthy?

"Buzzworthy is a digital agency model that has integrated marketing services within it. The majority of my clients are coming to me for digital placement and management. We have search engine optimization, social media management, content marketing, and digital ad placement and management. When people can move their budget past that, maximizing the digital realm, then I have the experience to get them then the complimentary mass media or what we consider traditional media, maybe integrating radio or TV. We have tools that show whether or not, and how much, traditional media moves the needle. We have ways of syncing up when a spot is run and then watching any movement in a date after that time frame to monitor its effects. We're combining digital marketing's measurability with traditional marketing to assess whether there's as much ROI as we were getting with just digital.

Buzzbizz Media is a holding company now, and Buzzbizz Studios is a production studio. The audio and video production feeds the other divisions when they need it. I have teams specifically doing audio/video and a team working for me in the Buzzworthy Integrated Marketing realm. I have a dedicated team for the Better Than Hosting, and a dedicated team for Color Theory Design & Prints - which is that graphic design division."

How did you figure out how to make that all happen? Did you have a formal business degree, or did you just figure it out along the way? Did you use mentors?

"I've had a few mentors over the years. Entrepreneurship is all about figuring it out. If somebody is not willing to get their hands dirty and have things go wrong five different ways before it goes right, they should never own their own business. If you need books that tell you exactly how to do everything, get a franchise model. That will show you how to be in business. Even then, every business is different. Even in the franchise model, every location is different. Clients are different. It's all trial and error.

In my late thirties, I went back to school to get my bachelor's degree in small business management and entrepreneurship. I didn't learn much in getting my degree except that you don't need your degree to be an entrepreneur. There's plenty of millionaires out there that will show you that it's possible to succeed in business without a formal degree. Can you be a smarter business owner knowing some of the things you're going to learn from a degree? Yes. Do you have to wait four years to get that kind of information? No. There's so much information on the internet right now. You could probably learn everything you need to know in about 90 days and feel comfortable enough to move forward.

The one thing that I did learn in the new iterations of my business is that building an expansive, detailed business plan is almost a waste of time, unless you're trying to get funding. If you're self-funding with sweat equity and money that you saved, a short business plan centered around your situation is much more valuable and about all you need.

Building a marketing plan is the part people don't do enough of. Marketing is what builds a small business. Unfortunately, I have worked with so many businesses that come to me without a marketing plan. I've worked with 78 international companies and over 500 small to medium-sized companies over the last 15 years. During that time, I've seen the last thing startups budget and plan for is marketing. They think the business will just take off and do its thing. Build it and they will come type of mentality. But in reality, it's just the opposite. Is there a market?

Market research is the first thing people should be doing. Then they should be figuring out how much it's going to cost to bring the product or service to market. Then reverse engineer everything. What is it going to take to run a business that will support that marketing? Then move forward. Then you have a full budget for your marketing, and you know how long your runway is once you get funding."

In a time when a lot of small businesses are rushing to digital, how do you argue the value of traditional marketing for small business owners who have a limited budget?

"The first thing we do is take a look at what they're doing and how those tactics are working or not. When it comes to a small business, everything depends on their budget. There's so much you can do with a small budget in digital that you can't do in traditional. The majority of the time, I argue towards traditional when there needs to be an integration. That integration, nine times out of ten, comes when you have maximized the value, or ROI, of social media.

Say you have a company that has to educate people about their product. It's not an automatic product. So, you've got something new coming to the market, and you're going to spend a lot of time educating the general public. That's when mass media can help you in getting that impression. It all has to push back to interaction with inbound marketing, which is back to the digital side. TV viewership and radio listening are up right now, so there are more radio stations to choose from. You can niche your market better. Now with cable cutting, you can just choose one type of network and get a wider spread. You don't have to be as localized in getting that reach.

When we talk about traditional marketing, the lines are getting blurred now because TV and radio have become apps themselves. All of the major networks have their own streaming apps. There's a lot of new ways of utilizing what we could consider traditional on a digital platform. The argument is not as much of an argument as it is a new philosophy and a fresh attack on the same medium."

Do you think successful entrepreneurs are born or made?

"You can argue that either way. There's a personality type that's more prone to entrepreneurship. Conversely, certain personality traits don't lend themselves to entrepreneurship. Then your upbringing affects your ability to be an entrepreneur. So, it's a little bit of both. It's like a thoroughbred horse. They're born with a lot of good traits. But unless that horse goes through all of the training it takes to be a champion thoroughbred, they'll just be another horse. The process of becoming an entrepreneur is taught at the school of hard knocks. The desire comes first. If you have all the traits and no desire - then, you'll never be an entrepreneur. The desire comes first and then the resilience, which is one of those traits that you need. As long as all that holds true, then the school of hard knocks creates and trains that entrepreneur."

Tell me about the pivotal roadblocks you experienced on your way to becoming a successful business owner.

"I never thought I was a successful business owner, and that was probably my first roadblock. I was playing small for a long time. I had big dreams, but I was not leveraging my talents as a leader. But then, once that came to fruition, and I learned my power as a leader.

The hurdles that entrepreneurs will inevitably hit regardless of what industry they're in will have to do with the manpower or the workforce they have around them. We can all sit there and ask to have the best people-

people who are smarter than us in all the areas we are weak. But people are inevitably selfish and flaky in general. It's challenging for anybody to have the passion you have as an entrepreneur for your business.

Everyone's left with a diamond in the rough. At some point, the people around you will be the ones that will let you down before you quit. Understand that and put the processes in place to inevitably exercise the turnover that will happen. It's not if it will happen. It's when it will happen. Because life happens. People move, die, retire, change their careers, or start their own businesses. The people you have today will most likely not be the people you have in front of you working on that business in two to five years.

The biggest hurdle is the workforce because the landscape of the workforce has changed so much. Remote working, flexible work hours, and flexible workspace adds to that. Kids get out of school nowadays to have three different jobs that all pay more than the next one, and if it doesn't move fast enough or according to whatever timeline they have in their head, they just go to the next job. When I look at resumes and see a six-month stint somewhere more than once, I know there's no way I'll hire the person. Even if they sit there and tell me how they're ready to settle down and this is what they want. The truth is, they don't know what they want yet. Entrepreneurs don't have the luxury of retraining people all the time. Turnover costs so much money and creates so many barriers to your growth.

Self-doubt can also be a massive barrier for an entrepreneur. It's a pretty lonely track in the beginning. When two business owners become partners, you're less lonely. But partnerships can either be a blessing or a curse. I tend to think of them as a 'blessed curse.' Two heads are better than one, but you have to agree on things to move forward. It slows things down for better or for worse.

And, of course, your cash flow. Cash is king. If there's one thing I could tell my younger self, it's to hold on to money and just stuff it away for rainy days or new opportunities. There are so many times I saw a new opportunity that I didn't have enough cash flow to take full advantage of. And bigger is not always better."

How has entrepreneurship affected your personal life?

"When I was a young entrepreneur, I was 'blessed' with a recent divorce. I could dive right into my business and work 18 hours a day, so I didn't have to deal with the personal side. Eventually, I realized all work no play makes for a dull boy. It also makes for a broken heart. If you can find somebody who can celebrate your losses as well as they celebrate your successes, it becomes much less lonely. When you're doing it yourself, you're the only one who sees what needs to happen. Nobody else around you does. And you can't befriend your employees. You can be friendly with them and support them and their families, but you have to stay at an arms distance to make wise business decisions that are not impeded by emotion. Once you put emotion into the business, your business becomes a house of cards.

As far as relationships go, work-life balance is one of the most important things an entrepreneur can tackle early on. It's easy to do your hack-a-thons and spend twelve to eighteen hours a day working on the business. But you've got to create an infrastructure that'll allow you to walk away from it because you need time for yourself. You also eventually need to be able to sell your business. But if you don't set up the right infrastructure, you can work yourself into exhaustion and burn out. You need to build in breathing room for you to be human. Studies show you need to have just as much time off as any employee out there. You might work hard, but you have to play hard, too.

I just took five days off to be with an old friend from California, and we got off the grid and unplugged as much as possible. I think I checked my email twice in five days and took two calls in that whole time. Anything else would be there when I get back. People get so wound up thinking if they miss this one opportunity, it's all going to go away. No, there's more opportunity than you can handle. Be okay with that and keep that life balance because it's a journey, not a destination.

Once you get to that point and hit that goal, all you've done is hit a mile marker in a long journey, and you're going to create another goal right behind it. As you come to it, you're going to be creating goals past that too. That's never going to end. You need to know that and make sure you're putting yourself first, along with your family and the people you love. Make sure that they come first. Your business needs that. Then you work to live, not live to work."

How do you handle negativity or naysayers in your business or in your life?

"It's funny - we talk about an entrepreneur's resilience, but there's a fine line between being stubborn and being an idiot. Entrepreneurs are known for not taking 'no' for an answer. I know guys who used to say, 'No' is not 'no' forever. Just 'no' today.' They think that means 'I have to come back at a different angle or different process and try it again'. Or, 'maybe if I just keep asking a question, you will finally just say 'yes." Understanding the difference between just not seeing reality and actual negativity is important.

When dealing with negativity, you will only allow it in your life when you're not one hundred percent sure of where you're going. You need that negativity to feed your doubts so you can feel okay about your doubts. If you find negativity around you, you need to find ways to get rid it.

Being an entrepreneur, you need to have a very short-term memory in this area. It's just like in sports where you have that quarterback throw that stupid throw that just gets picked up. You're like, 'Damn it, I didn't mean to do that. I don't know why I did that. I know better than to do that.' Then 25 seconds later, guess what? He's in the huddle and has to make those same decisions again. He has to forget what just happened 25 seconds ago. Athletes like that have to learn from their mistakes and know how to read it as a mistake. But then they have to forget that it happened because that fear of that failure will cripple and kill them. Entrepreneurs need the same type of short-term memory.

There are many times I've attacked something, thinking it's going to work even though everybody tells me it won't. But as I get it out there, it works for a minute – and then it completely fails. Normal people would recognize that it didn't work and move on to something else that will. An entrepreneur says, 'Okay, that didn't work the way I wanted it to. We're going to take the same ball and try to throw it a different way to see if we can get it to bounce the way we want it to.'

You have to celebrate your losses, rejections, 'no's', and negativity. You have to ask yourself what you're learning from them instead of letting them break you down. People's rejection is just their perception of what they don't understand or agree with. So, you have to say, 'Okay, we don't see eye-to-eye. I'm either going try to see your perspective or move on.' If you do that every time, it does not affect you because you don't allow it. It's just part of the process. But if you can't sit there and think, 'Oh, I suck because they don't like me,' or 'I suck because they didn't say agree,' or 'I suck because I didn't get that RFP.' No. It's just what you put out there was not the right fit at the time, or you weren't ready for that yet.

When rejection happens, you need to learn why it happened and build upon that. The next time that opportunity comes up, you can either decide that you don't care about that type of project or don't want to deal with that type of person. Or maybe you do want that project and are ready because you've learned from it. You built upon it, and now you have an offer. Then you put a different type of RFP together, and all of a sudden, you're getting the projects that you're looking for. If you use rejection and negativity as building blocks to success instead of hurdles to success, you will never be affected by negativity."

What keeps you going through the hard times?

"Well, I've found out there's no such thing as easy times. It's always a challenge being an entrepreneur because there's no coasting in owning a business. It comes back to resilience, your passion for what you're doing, and how much you believe in what you're doing. That's why people who run a business for the money don't last as long as people who do it for passion. If resilience and passion are the ingredients for not quitting, the pursuit of continued success is the outcome of those ingredients.

This is a job, and everybody has hard jobs. It doesn't matter if you're punching a time clock. You have a job to do. When the going gets tough, the tough get going. Either you get another job, or you figure out the struggle that you're going through at that moment. Then you get through it and grow from it. It goes back to negativity and rejection. You can be a product of circumstance and allow circumstance to run you. Or you can own circumstance and find ways to profit from it."

Would you say your military experience has affected how you run your business? How so?

"I'm a third-generation Air Force. My grandfather was in WWII, my parents were both in the Air Force and served in the Vietnam War era, and then I served for ten years just before I started Buzzbizz in 2005. One of the things you learn in the military is discipline and the respect of rank. In the civilian world, there's a lack of that respect. In the military, you don't give respect until it is earned. As a leader, that is so important. Rank doesn't guarantee respect – in business or in life. You have to earn it.

I've had commanders in the Air Force who knew that I was good at what I did, and they respected that. They showed me respect when they didn't need to. But as great leaders, they knew that respect would motivate me to work hard and improve my skill set. With that training, mentality, and perspective, I've always tried to do the same for my employees and the people I work with. If you're better, that just makes the organization better. I want to make people better. It's hard work to make things happen and to improvise and overcome.

In the military, I was aircrew. When you're in the air, you figure stuff out. You improvise, overcome, adapt, and make things happen in a moment. And that's true in entrepreneurship. Work ethic, respect, and ingenuity all play into the success of an entrepreneur. I know a lot of guys who've gotten out and have been very successful. But they had to get over the paychecks not being there every two weeks like they are when you're in the military."

Looking back, is there anything you would have done differently throughout your journey so far?

"Yes. I think the business had to start where it was so I could grow into it. I don't think I would start my business any differently because that was where my passion was. It allowed me to build a business that I could grow into, mature into. Because it takes a certain level of maturity to grow and scale a business. Guys like Mark Zuckerberg, their businesses grew past them very early. They've made some huge mistakes that they'll never be able to take back because the business grew faster than they could grow.

There was a time where I'd put caps on my growth. I'd make a goal and say, 'we're going to grow to this point.' Then, at that point, I'd have to reevaluate how business was and decided whether we could take on more growth. I'd decide if I wanted the growth, and if I did, I'd figure out what it was going to take to continue to be successful. Because the business changes, and it doesn't scale in a linear fashion. Some things take less effort, and other things take more effort. When you get bigger, you have more opportunities for waste and margin of error, which until you get that big, you don't see.

But if I could do it all over again, I'd hire slower and fire faster. That's one of the biggest things I've learned in honing people for the last 15 years. I had a propensity to try to groom people too much. I believe it's good to hire for potential, but they must have what it takes to do the job you're hiring them for. I made too many hires based on attitude and not aptitude. My hiring practices could have definitely been different over the years, which would have put me in a different position."

If you were talking to somebody who is thinking about starting their own business, what's one piece of advice you would offer them?

"It depends on who it is and where they're at in life. It's different for everybody. If they've been working for a long time, I would tell them to make sure they have the money to go into business. And to have the reserves in their private coffers to outlast twice as long as they think it's going to take for their business to take off.

If somebody is borrowing money to start their business, I'd say they need to budget three to four times as much as they think it's going to take. I'm not kidding - three to four times as much as you think it's going to take. I don't care how much you sharpen that pencil. It always takes more than you think. It's going to take energy, time, and money. Period. End of story. I have seen very few businesses able to get to achieve success under budget. Very, very few. Just as few get it with even double the budget they were looking at. More often, I see three to four times their budget and time estimate. I've seen a very seasoned business owner who thought he would be able to build-out his product in three to six months. I came in only to find out it took him three months to figure out what they were doing. Now it's going to take him another six months to build it out. Running a startup is unpredictable like that.

For somebody who is young and coming out of school, I'd say make sure that the business that you're going into it for the passion of what you're providing versus the lifestyle that you're yearning for."

You did a lot of bootstrapping in your business, especially in the early years. How did you figure out that process, and what did you learn from that?

"You have to be good at projection, creating a stairway off of the small successes, and understanding it is a very long road. When you're climbing stairs, it takes a lot of energy, and you run out of breath. When you're running a marathon, it's usually flat ground, so once you get in a groove, it's really easy to do. When you're trying to grow something, you're climbing stairs versus running across the plain. Every step is one step. You need to take it one step at a time and not get too far ahead of yourself. That is one of the most important things.

When you're running an agency, people are your most significant expense. When we were doing $1.2 million in revenue, I had almost $900,000 in payroll in that year. That's not the building expenses or anything else. That's just salaries, taxes, and benefits. When you're growing, you have to take a look at the people you have and how far you can scale with those people. Then you have to take a look at the cost of bringing on the next person because when they come on, they're usually at a deficit. They're not profitable until you get them to certain percentage of prime or leverage. When you're scaling an agency, you're usually trading time for money. That's the magic potion that you have to figure out.

Trying to find ways to automate as many things as possible for the number of people you have versus adding more people is the key. It's a tool we didn't have ten years ago. There are so many tools now that you can use to eliminate the need for as many people. An agency can run leaner and meaner. We're seeing it across the nation. You don't need 1500 people to run an agency anymore. You can probably run that same size of agency for about a third of the people. It becomes more of how many people are forward-facing versus doing technician jobs.

When you are bootstrapping, it's better to do more with fewer people. You need to put reserves away. You cannot bootstrap yourself off of the immediate revenue that you're getting while you're growing. You need to be in a place where you're able to have funds set aside so that you have seed money for that next pull. I did that very poorly early on. I assumed because money was coming in, it was always going to come in. So I thought I could use that money to run the business. I should have been holding to my budget and putting away any extra money that came in. That way, if I had a bad month, I could still maintain the budget. I could pull from the reserves.

One of the books that I read recently by Mike Michalowicz, *Profit First,* teaches you how to pull aside your profit first, rather than income minus cost equal profit. It's income minus profit equals operation budget. When you're paying yourself first and using the rest for operations, it teaches you how to bootstrap yourself better. For instance, If I want to hire another person, I have to consider if I can afford it without sacrificing my income. If the answer is 'no,' I either have to reduce my operations cost or increase sales to have a bigger budget to hire someone. That's how you bootstrap, and it's the only way to do it.

Many people will bootstrap themselves on the high months and immediately find themselves in a deficit upon a lousy month. I did something like that the four or five years in the beginning. I somehow made it through, but that's because it was a big push upwards. I was building this giant house of cards, thinking that everything will fall into place if we can just get to this point. That's not measured growth. That's growing too fast for growth's sake. That's when it all comes crashing down. That foundation is built on cash flow. You have to ask yourself tough questions, like 'if no money came in for the next 30 days, would I be able to pay everybody's salary and all the bills?' You should have two to three months in reserve before you decide to grow a little bit more. Then just make that next step, one step at a time."

What advice would you offer to somebody who is thinking about throwing in the towel?
"I've done that once. I have had friends who were business owners, and

their businesses were failing. So they'd say to me, 'I have to get a job, but I'm un-hirable.' I didn't understand what they were talking about. I'd say, 'What do you mean you're un-hirable? You're a leader, and you've done all this stuff.' They'd say, 'Yeah, but I've owned my business. I haven't had a job in 20 years.' That never clicked with me until there was a time when I thought I didn't want to do it anymore. I didn't want to run the business that way anymore, and that's the only business model I knew then. So I started thinking, 'What if I just become a CMO? I can make just as much money as I'm trying to make now with 40- or 50- hour workweeks.' Then I started looking at people who have executive jobs and what their lifestyle looks like. I decided that wasn't for me.

One thing I found is that you don't get freedom from being an entrepreneur. People are like, 'I'm going to be my own boss!' But you're not your own boss. Multiply the number of clients you have by one, and that's how many bosses you have. So, get a hundred clients, and have a hundred bosses. Sure, you have the freedom to choose who to work for. You have the freedom to decide how you work, and you have the freedom to choose poorly if you want. And, you have to understand that there are repercussions to that.

When you go from that mindset to working for somebody else, you take away that freedom. That freedom is very elusive. And sometimes, we get dragged down. You hear that saying, 'an entrepreneur will work 60 hours a week to avoid a 40-hour week job,' and that's because you have the freedom to make those decisions. Freedom that you wouldn't have working for somebody else, regardless of what kind of latitude they say they're going to give you.

The other thing is that you're then reducing the amount of financial independence that you have. As an entrepreneur, I can decide I need a certain amount of money, and then I can go back to my business to figure out how to pull that money out. You can't do that with a job. Unless you're in sales. But once you're going to go to sales, you're restricting how much you can make. Entrepreneurship gives you significant freedom, which is something we tend to forget when times are hard."

Is there anything that we haven't covered that you want to add?

"Owning your own business is all about being willing to accept reality as it comes. You can only steer your fortune so much. As entrepreneurs, we envision what it's going to look like, and we need that vision because it's what we keep our eyes focused on. It's what keeps us moving a lot of the time. But as we're going towards what we think we're going to do, the ability to have peripheral vision to pick up on other cues helps. You can see that you might be going in the wrong direction and make those adjustments to shift towards a more prosperous path. But that's a talent that takes time and patience to build. Any entrepreneur that's successful would probably agree with that statement. You have to be open to reality.

It's one thing to say 'no' to the naysayers. It's another thing to say, 'Despite what all the indications say, I shouldn't be able to do it. But I'm going to do anyway.' I get that. That's trailblazing. But even then, keeping your head on a swivel and looking at the environment around you allows you to make logical and informed business decisions along the way. You'll be able to steer your business to places that you never thought you would be able to go.

I would have never thought that I'd be happier producing a quarter of what I was two years ago. I would never have believed you if you'd told me, 'You're not going to be bringing in $2.2 million, but you're going to be four times happier bringing in a quarter of the money. And your profit margin will be higher too.' I would never have understood that. As things progressed, I realized I didn't like being a CEO. I didn't want to be a CEO anymore. I wanted to be an entrepreneur again. I owned a job at that point instead of being an innovator and creator. My friends and loved ones tell me, 'You're so much happier than you were just a year ago.' I have more freedom now to do the things I want to do. I have more money now, even though my gross revenue is one-quarter of what it was. It's not the money. You have to do your passion. If you're doing it for the money, you'll fail. If you follow the passion, you'll be where you're supposed to be. And it's very rarely how you think it's going to be."

8 STRATEGY SESSION: GROWING WITH PURPOSE

Before you read on, I want you to close your eyes and visualize a successful business. Got it? Great! Chances are, the successful business that first popped into your head has revenue in the millions or billions. It likely has hundreds to thousands of employees and sits on the Fortune 500 list every year. It may be publicly traded, and everyone knows the brand nationwide. The owner has a big house (or multiple big houses), a shiny new car, and vacations in exotic locales every year.

We hear a lot of talk about scaling a business – the bigger you can grow, the better. However, not every business is suited for scalability. More importantly, not every business owner will be fulfilled scaling to a multi-million-dollar company. There is certainly nothing wrong with having high-revenue goals. After all, revenue does keep the lights on in any business. However, a clear direction is more vital to longevity than a blind push for money.

One of the reasons I asked Buzz to sit for an interview is to get his perspective on scaling quickly versus managing growth with intention. As you've likely gathered from the interview, Buzz has a quintessential entrepreneur personality - he's very driven, very goal-oriented, and very growth-focused. So it's interesting to hear him say, "Wait, there's a smarter way to do this." In my work with entrepreneurs throughout the years, I've seen many find themselves in the same situation where Buzz found himself. So hearing his story is helpful because you get to see someone adapt and find success on their own terms.

Entrepreneurs are competitive by nature. We like to win. We want to be the best. Many of us will run ourselves ragged to accomplish this. Before you find yourself sucked into the race to revenue, take a moment, and do some introspection. Defining what success means for you and your unique business can mean the difference between finding joy in your process and burning out. After all, you will not make it to any finish line if you cannot handle the marathon. The good news is, you get to choose your path.

What Happens if You Grow Too Quickly?

Before we talk about defining success and establishing your plan for purposeful growth, let's talk about the dangers of growing too quickly. According to the Small Business Administration, only about 50% of companies survive past their first five years, and only about 33% survive more than ten years. Out of these, the most common reason for small business failure is cash flow issues. Cash flow involves the money coming in versus the money going out and the timing of that rotation.

Here's an example of how that can tank a business faster than any other issue. Let's say that you own a service-based business. In that service-based business, you have $200,000 in monthly invoices. Congratulations! If this is an average month for you, you are on track to make more than $2 million this year! You're a success, right? Not so fast. That $200,000 is a significant number, but how long does it take you to collect that $200,000? More importantly, do you have enough cash in your accounts to cover essentials – like payroll – in the meantime? Falling behind on vendor payments and rent can increase your overhead cost in late fees. Falling behind on payroll carries a much harsher punishment. You would be surprised how many service-based businesses report high revenues but cannot pay their bills month to month. So, rather than scaling, they close their doors, often leaving their owners with substantial debt.

My intent is not to talk you out of reaching millions or even billions in revenue as quickly as possible. By all means, reach for the stars! If that is truly your goal, I hope you succeed. If you struggle with justifying a goal to find an alternative path, I hope that you read through Buzz's story and gain some insight into the benefit of growing sustainably and with intention. I also hope that you drop any guilt you may have if you do not want to devote your legacy to hitting a certain revenue level within a set timeframe. There are a variety of other ways you can make an impact as a business owner.

Defining Success for You

There is no wrong answer to the question: "What does success look like to you?" So why are we continually trying to stuff ourselves into the stereotypical "entrepreneur" version of success? The reality is success can mean something different for every business owner. Perhaps your goal is to make millions. Maybe your goal is to be a job creator. Alternatively, you may want to serve your community with a unique product. Or, your goal may be just to create a sustainable income and financial freedom for your family. All of these are worthwhile goals for a business.

Whether you are considering starting your business or struggling to keep going in your current business, learning to define your goals without guilt is the first step. It doesn't matter what anyone else's version of success might be. You need to dig into the real reason you started your company and be okay with that. Once you define your personal goals for your business, you can craft your business plan around those goals. Otherwise, you're going to try and fit your business plan into what you think your goals should be, which will drive you to burnout and disillusionment in the process.

Build Your Plan

I briefly touched on writing a business plan in a previous chapter, so now I want to expand on that with a lens of lean growth at the focus. Buzz mentioned in his interview that creating that detailed business plan didn't help him. It was the smaller, to-the-point business plan that empowered him to solidify his direction in the revamped business model he chose. From my experience, many business owners get tangled up in the business planning process when it's just not necessary unless you are seeking outside funding. There is a misunderstanding that a business plan requires hours of work, numerous financial projects, and general tedium. When you are growing a lean business, you don't necessarily need all of that because you are less likely to be asking for commercial funding. You just need the basic layout of your business, why it matters to your market, and how you are going to make money.

In fact, you can knock out a business plan in less than two hours. Pull your profit and loss statements, your current sales projections, your existing cash flow budget, and take a moment to answer the following questions:

What problem does my product or service solve?
How does my product or service solve this problem?
Who is most likely to purchase this product or service?
How does this audience make decisions on making purchases?
What are three ways for me to reach that audience right now?
How much does it cost to produce/perform my product or service?
What are my financial goals for the next year, three years, and five years?

The purpose of these questions is to help you clearly define your business vision. To grow with purpose, you need to have a fixed "north star." Something to keep you on the right path. A simple business plan exercise like this provides something for you to look to as you make decisions. Once you've answered these questions, you are better prepared to define your marketing budget, staffing needs, and how to improve your sales in the most cost-efficient way possible while staying true to your goals.

Gather Your Resources

Now that you have defined your goals and established a plan, it becomes easier to establish which resources will be the best investment for your business. You need to strive to surround yourself with people and processes who will keep you in check and on the right road to reaching your goals. Keep in mind that one of the keys to success in growing sustainably is maintaining a balance between what you can outsource, what you can automate, and what you need to do yourself.

One of the best things you can do to help your business is to hire a bookkeeper. Regardless of your industry, this needs to be your first investment. As entrepreneurs, we tend to be big picture people. Sometimes, that means that we cannot see potential risks regarding cash flow and money management. Hiring a certified public accountant (CPA) and a bookkeeper can help you create a path for success.

Of course, it's essential to keep in mind that things will change along the way. An advisor can help you make appropriate adjustments to your strategy as your business grows and recommend opportunities to improve efficiency before you find yourself in a tough spot with cash flow. Look for someone who isn't afraid to push back on you when you want to spend money. You need someone capable of bringing you back to sanity when you get "shiny object" syndrome and try to take on too much too soon.

I frequently make the argument that it has never been easier to own or start a business – yes, even in the middle of a pandemic in 2020. We have an environment that small business owners before us never had access to – that is, the world of attainable automation. Between customer relationship management (CRM) software, ecommerce platforms, invoicing tools, marketing software, and even employee management apps, the opportunities for a more cost-efficient business process have never been greater. The key to success is balance. You do not want to be so far removed from the personal connection in your business that everything is done via computer, but there are facets of every part of your business that can be streamlined. This leaves the door open for you to spend your time building your business, not working on the day-to-day. It also creates an environment where your employees can be focused more on revenue-generating tasks, not just busywork.

An important consideration when growing a business is deciding to take on employees. It is important to note that payroll is often the highest overhead costs for businesses. Salaries or hourly pay, insurance, taxes, and associated fees add up quickly for quality employees. These items, in addition to turnover costs, add up even faster for bad employees. In fact, turnover costs in American businesses added up to more than $600 billion in 2018 alone (The Work Institute, 2020). As Buzz noted in his interview, learning to hire and develop the right employees substantially impacted his business. To grow with purpose, you must learn how to hire well.

Moreover, you need to have an established and efficient training program to ensure that your new team member can succeed in your business's culture. Finally, never hire an employee without a management plan. You need to be engaged with your team, understand their needs and goals, and create a mutually beneficial environment to keep them in your business. As they should be, employees are selfish, and you have to give them a good reason to stay. Otherwise, the employees you need to run your business will bury your company in overhead costs. If you are struggling with managing employees, it may be worthwhile to hire a human resources consultant to help you succeed.

Learn, Grow, Adapt

Whether your goal is managed growth or rapid scalability, you cannot remain stagnant in your business. To be a business owner is to stay in a constant state of adaptability. Hard truth: if that's not you, you may want to consider another field of work. There are so many facets of entrepreneurship that we cannot control but directly impact our businesses. Examples include the economy, the political climate, generational shifts in consumers, regulatory compliance requirements, tax rates, natural disasters or pandemics, and so on. Even if you want to stay small, you will need to be the type of leader who can make the hard decisions swiftly and with a positive attitude. It's a lot of pressure. The good news is, most of the time, it's also a lot of fun.

Create a set time every month, quarter, and year to check your progress toward your goals. It doesn't matter what those goals are – make sure you are making at least a little progress every month. If you aren't making progress, then you have an opportunity to improve your business processes. Where is the issue, and how can you correct it? This is where having an accountant or CPA can help you with objective analysis.

As you grow, you may find that your business's natural changes don't match your personal goals. Take regular inventory of your joy in running your business and your personal life. If your goal is to stay small but build a comfortable life for yourself or your family, creating a situation where you are working 100 hours a week to keep up with customer demand may be frustrating and not a reason to celebrate. Before you reach the point of burnout, check in with yourself and your family to decide where your ceiling needs to be, if it needs to exist at all. Talk to your CPA to determine if you can afford to hire a new employee, allowing you greater work-life balance. Maybe consider adjusting your plan or scaling down on your niche market. If you aren't taking care of yourself and your family, you're not going to sustain yourself in business. Honesty is essential here, and there is no wrong answer. You may think you can manage the unhappiness for a short time, but the moment you allow your business to control your life, and not the other way around, it's incredibly hard to regain control. The fact is, you also risk hurting what you've built in your company and your personal life.

Above all, never be afraid to ask for advice. Somewhere along the line, entrepreneurs decided we needed to know everything about running a business to be successful. This misconception is ironic because most of us only know fragments of different aspects of running a business. So, having a business mentor can be helpful here. You need an objective third party – not a friend or family member – who can take the emotion out of an issue and help you navigate a sustainable path forward. Many times, that's the best way to get yourself out of feeling stuck. You just need to find a mentor or advisor who can hold you accountable while making you comfortable enough to be completely honest with them. If you do not have a mentor, I recommend reaching out to organizations like SCORE, your local Small Business Development Center, or your Small Business Administration office. They will likely direct you to local sources of business mentors that will fit your needs.

If you are still unable to find a mentor, I personally welcome you to reach out to my team directly on firstdollarfeeling.com, and we will assist you in finding a no-cost mentor who will meet your needs.

KEY TAKEAWAYS

KEY TAKEAWAYS

KEY TAKEAWAYS

9 COURTNEY WOLFE, RENTWISE PROPERTY MANAGEMENT

Courtney Wolfe has been an entrepreneur from a relatively young age. However, her path to success has taken a series of twists and turns, making it an excellent case study for entrepreneurs in various stages of business. Courtney is a very hands-on type of businesswoman, which allows her to offer excellent insight into different ways to build a business. In fact, she's launched businesses in three different industries so far. This is Courtney's story.

How long have you been an entrepreneur?

"I bought a coffee shop when I was 26, and it was my first business. I had a regular job just like everyone else, and I was a single mom with a couple of kids. I had been working for someone else pretty much all my life. I knew I wanted something different and didn't want to work for anyone else. My father helped me by co-signing on a loan for the shop. But I did everything else. I created my required business plan, from purchasing to profit and loss. I handled it all myself. It was the most essential learning lesson of my entire life. It was super rad and incredibly terrifying to sit in front of a banker, but I did it - and I got a small business loan.

About two years later, Dutch Brothers Coffee purchased the shop from me. After that, my sister needed help in her real estate business. With no background, I decided that I would dive into photography and become a real estate photographer. It turned out that I was pretty good at it. I was approached shortly after about staging homes. I wasn't even sure what that meant, so I did a lot of research and started offering staging and design for

78

real estate agents along with my photography. About that time, a company called Tour Real Estate saw my work online and reached out to me, wondering if I wanted to work for them. They took a chance on me and taught me many valuable things, like how to use Photoshop.

Shortly after that, I got pregnant. I decided to step away and take a break. Three and a half years later, another pregnancy, and then I remember shooting the Parade of Homes. I was eight and a half months pregnant with my youngest, carrying around an additional 50lbs of camera equipment. I just remember thinking how brutally hot it was.

The next business venture of mine happened was when my husband at the time was working for a sign shop. The owners wanted to sell and offered the shop to us. My husband at the time and I crunched some numbers and decided to move forward with a promissory note. I do not recommend doing this without some very particular attorneys involved. Those were a volatile couple of years. My husband and I ended up getting a divorce. I was 33, had three kids at home, and knew nothing about the sign business. I asked myself, 'What am I going to do? How will I support myself?'

I reached out to an old business broker colleague, and he told me about an opportunity he had. He knew of a property management company for sale, and he thought it would be a great fit. He took me to see it. When I walked in, I realized I happened to know the owners. They were clients of the sign shop that I owned at the time. Right then and there, they decided to sell it to me. They knew I was the right person; they trusted me. Within twelve days, I purchased another business – knowing nothing about how to run it. But it's how I got to where I am now."

And that property management company is RentWise Property Management, your current business. How long have you owned RentWise?

"I closed on it on my 34th birthday, in 2012. So, that's eight years."

So you had some understanding of the real estate market from the staging and the photography side of the business. How did you handle that learning curve as you jumped into full property management?

"Well, probably not the best way, but I'm a researcher. Google was my best friend, and I leaned on my intuition. I'm a very driven person. When I need to know something, I find the answers. But the learning curve was brutal. I closed on a Thursday on a 38-door property account. Then on that

Friday, I was fired by a lady with five properties. I cried a lot. I thought, 'Oh my gosh. What am I going to do?' It was so easy to lose that income. I didn't know any of these people. They didn't know me. I felt like I wasn't doing things right, and I had no idea what I was doing. I wasn't sure how to make it. Then Monday came, and I woke up around seven in the morning to a voice mail from a tenant whose kitchen had flooded. I had no idea what to do. No idea. I didn't even know who to call. So, I called the owner of the home. I told him what had happened; I tried to sound as smart as possible on the phone with him. He told me exactly who he wanted me to call. Then, I just started to follow the breadcrumbs.

Another thing that worked was making decisions about each property as if it were my own home. I'd ask myself, 'What would I want done in this instance?' That led me to see that I was quite good at this. I like to call myself a 'crisis negotiator.' Every day after that was a new call and a new lesson. It's always a new adventure. For three years, I was on my own, with the help of a part-time employee who kept the business afloat while I ran the company. Eventually, I found a tribe of people to help me, and that changed everything."

Do you have formal business training?

"I was a high school dropout. I learned everything the hard way. That was my training. My dad recently passed away, and honestly, I attribute much of my success to him. He taught my sister Wendy and me to take care of ourselves. No matter what it took. I sure didn't make my life the easiest it could have been. But when it came to taking care of my children and myself, I was determined to do it right. My dad believed in us every step of the way, and we had an extensive family support system. So, I'm guessing that it helped a ton. I did drop out and get my GED. I tried to go to college, but it didn't work. It was so hard with kids and stuff. We are just really driven people. I tell you, that's one reason I went out on my own. We are very driven.

Another reason I also went into entrepreneurship on my own is for the freedom. I'll never forget my son's football game when he was in sixth grade. I was 26, and I had a regular day job. The game started at 4:00 p.m., and I didn't get off until 5:00 p.m. I asked to leave early, but I couldn't. By the time I got there, the game was almost over. I just sat in my car and cried. I felt like such a failure as a mom. I remember him looking so disappointed, even though he knew it wasn't my fault. I decided then that I would never let someone else have a say in whether I could be at my kid's game again. I went home that night, found a business that I thought I could run well, and called my dad. I gave my two weeks' notice two days later. A month and a half later, we got approval from the bank. Then 15 days after that, I owned the coffee shop. It had happened so fast, but I had no fear."

Let's talk about that first coffee shop for a moment. How did you feel when you first started making money in the business?

"Oh, gosh, I felt super proud. But I was terrified. I could almost have peed in my pants. I wasn't even sure how to make a latte. But, I just knew that I would figure it all out. I just knew. I also knew that if it didn't work out, there would be another plan."

Eventually, you sold your shop to Dutch Brothers – a much larger coffee company. Tell me about that experience.

"Oh, yeah, that was crazy. I bought this coffee shop, and I wasn't making very much money with it. I was borrowing money from my dad to get by and then paying him back when I could.

There was major construction starting in the area. The city was building a 10-mile overpass right by us. But I wasn't smart enough to look into it beforehand, so I didn't think about the impact it would have on us. Then six months in, Dutch Brothers randomly asked me if I wanted to sell. I very confidently turned the offer down. I mean, I thought I was doing great. I was almost offended that they even asked me if I wanted to sell. Their representative left, and I didn't see him again.

A year and a half passed, and I tried to make it work. But it's tough when you don't have money to market or an existing brand to lean on. It's a struggle, and I worked my butt off. I had to bring my oldest daughter, Zoe, with me when I went to work each day because I couldn't afford daycare. One of my customers made a TV shelf in the backroom, and that's where she would hang out every day. Zoe is 19 now, but I have some really fond memories of her giving out cookies and stirring the lemonade for the customers.

Eventually, I realized that this wasn't an ideal situation for me. The shop was not going to support me, and I didn't have the capital to put into it to make it bigger. My sister was able to put it on the market as her first commercial deal. Four hours after listing the shop, Jeff Yarnell, the founder of Dutch Brothers, showed up at my coffee shop window offering me $12,000 over the asking price. He told me I could take anything but the equipment with me and he would be back in three days. The day he came back, I left and never looked back. It was a great business to own, and it was one of my favorites."

After the coffee shop, you moved on to real estate photography, which played a big role in your current business. Tell me a little more about that venture.

"I had done some research on cameras, but again, I didn't know much. I took a photography class in the limited time that I was in college. But I loved it. I had to create a logo and build a brand. We did flyers, cold calls, and hoped to generate word of mouth referrals. Thank goodness I had that $12,000 over asking bid for the coffee shop. It alleviated a lot of stress in the beginning. I could pay off debt, so I had some breathing room while I got this up and going.

I started taking pictures for my sister, and she helped spread the word about my photography business. When the staging thing happened, it just fell into my lap. It was right before the housing market crashed. Everyone was outsourcing staging and photography. I reached out to a client that was always in the coffee shop, and he asked me if I wanted to stage their new model homes. I quoted him $1500 to stage a bedroom, kitchen, living room, and bathroom. I might have underbid that amount, but I knew that I was good at one thing. I was good at thrift shopping. I mean, I was stellar at thrift shopping. I could do stuff on the cheap because I was a single mom with two kids. I knew how to make a house look like a home for very little money. So I took his $1500, and I staged this house. He was amazed! He couldn't believe I made it happen. As a result, I began to stage all of his homes, and it kept me afloat.

I also did all the photography for those homes, and then it all kind of just melted together. That's when the gig with Tour Real Estate happened for me. I was an independent contractor. They had the branding and the clientele, and I got a steady stream of income from it. I did everything I wanted under their umbrella. It was quite perfect, and I could take Zoe with me if I wanted to. I believe one thing always leads to another. I went ahead and did that for about two and a half years."

You went on to purchase a sign company – an existing business – by financing directly from the owner versus using a traditional lender. I want to explore that a little bit because I know a lot of other prospective business owners consider that route, and it can become a big mess rather quickly. What was your experience with that kind of situation?

"I would never do it again just because I don't want to deal with it. But I think it could be done adequately with ethical parties, to be honest. I didn't make a promissory note when I sold it. We did it with an attorney and a purchase and sale agreement. But I wouldn't have known what an original purchase and sale agreement was unless I had done this with a promissory note. The way it works is the party selling the business says 'this is how much it costs', and then you agree to that. Then there's this ridiculously vague contract that you can download from the internet or even get from a lawyer is drawn up, and you sign it. I wouldn't do it again.

We made big mistakes. We agreed to purchase this company for well over market value. We knew when we were signing the agreement that it was too much. But at the time, we couldn't get a loan from the bank for that much money, so this was our best choice. We bought that company for $20,000 more than what it was worth. I thought the business had great potential. What I learned from this experience is how to research a company to see how it all works. I learned how to run a business with multiple employees. I also learned that both owners should know enough about all company areas, from bookkeeping to product production.

One day, a guy from the bank walked in with a camera and a file folder. He told us that they had a lien on everything we owned, and I needed to take inventory because I was in default. I had no clue what he was talking about. We didn't have a loan with them. I advised him of that and asked him to leave. I later found out that our promissory note was in the name of the original company. We had our own business name, and we only bought the assets of the original company - the customer list, the inventory that was in stock, and any pending orders. But we didn't buy the original company name, website, or anything else.

What I found out was the previous owners had started another company under a slightly different name, and they took the loan out in connection to the original company. My attorney advised us to stop paying them their monthly payments and instead deposit that amount in a savings account. He then informed us that the promissory note was null and void due to them selling the company to us under false pretenses. They claimed the company had no liens on it when it did indeed. It was a long battle. In the end, with all of our issues, I needed to cut my ties with this business. I wanted out.

By that time, my husband and I had divorced. I had purchased the property management company and was trying to run that. So I offered the business to our one employee for a fraction of what it was worth. I offered her the company 'as is' for $25,000. She went to the previous owners and told them about our offer. They agreed to make the necessary changes and move the note to her, so we were able to walk away debt-free."

By that time, you had been on quite a roller coaster in your businesses. When did you go from learning how to run this business to feeling confident that you had this under control?

"You know, I was a pretty resourceful girl. I was very good at delegating and surrounding myself with people who were good at what they did. I think that's one of the secrets of being an entrepreneur. I believe that people overthink how to be an entrepreneur. The truth is, the best kind of entrepreneurs are people who know how to find people to do what they need to do. It's all about delegation. I feel like surrounding yourself with people who are talented and skilled at what they do is essential. You cannot do everything, and we aren't good at everything. Surround yourself with people who are very good at what they do, and that is the best kind of entrepreneur.

To get better at running the business, I reached out to my friend, Misty, who owned a property management company. I asked her to lunch and just said: 'I need your help.' I asked her to sit down with me so I could ask her some questions. I needed help setting up bookkeeping because I was not familiar with the software. I was doing tutorials online, but they weren't helping. She knew a bookkeeper and offered to call her on my behalf.

Carly, the bookkeeper, came to my house and helped me set things up, and I hired her to help me once a month. Misty was so gracious to share Carly with me. I'm eternally grateful to her. Thanks to Carly's feedback and experience, I had time to do research and learn the business's ins and outs. I made new contacts, learned the ropes, and got a grasp on landlord-tenant and real estate law. That's when I began to feel more confident about running the business."

Looking back on all of your businesses, what have you found that worked (or didn't) on the marketing side?

"What works is hiring somebody who knows what they're doing. I didn't realize that what you did was an actual job. My entire life has been one significant learning experience. I believe networking matters. I don't do it as much now, but I spent the first three years consumed by it. You cannot grow any other way besides networking. You have to put the time in there. There might come a time when you grow enough that you don't have to do it as much. I still do business with the people I met through my networking groups. We are not only business friends but now social friends."

Can you expand on that? How did you leverage your network to grow your business?

"One thing that helped me be a better business owner is ensuring I could do every job before I hired someone else to do it. That helps me know what I need to delegate, who I need to hire, and what it will take to get the job done. That's part of being a business owner. Knowing what works and what doesn't work. It takes doing the work yourself for a little while. It makes all the difference.

I also found a tribe of property managers through NARPM®. NARPM® saved my life. I was drowning about four years ago. I hit a brick wall with my research and learning. I was unnecessarily reinventing the wheel with leases, policies, rules, and fees. NARPM® helped me improve my property management business. They could do that because they are a tribe of people who do what I do and want to help. Finding your tribe of people is another secret of success.

Some entrepreneurs might see others in their industry as competition, and the longer they see it that way, the more time they're wasting, without a doubt. There is so much to learn from one another. You're doing a disservice to others if you don't share. There is so much business to go around. As soon as you stop and look around and honestly give back, without any expectations, you will succeed. It will just happen. Everything will fall into place.

I didn't have to look hard for my tribe of people. It just accidentally found NARPM® one day when I was Googling something. Taking that opportunity to learn from them is what changed everything. It exponentially changed my life. You have to learn to let go of your ego. Open your mind and listen to what people have to say. Doing that will change everything. Entrepreneurs tend to be control freaks. Right? We know everything, and we don't need help. But that doesn't serve us at all. We need to humble ourselves a little bit and remember that we don't know everything. We are all just winging it most of the time.

A year and a half ago, I had a business coach remind me I needed to check my ego. I just always thought I was the boss. It was my job. It was what I did. He heard that, and he checked my ego in a way that I will be forever and eternally grateful for."

How do you handle negativity and naysayers as you've grown your

multiple businesses?

"I think your upbringing has a significant role in how you handle those negative moments. Having a great mindset and not caring for the most part is essential. I focus on believing what happens in my life is my responsibility. I was raised to know that everything that happens is in my control. Bad stuff happens to everyone. The sooner you realize that walking around allowing yourself to be offended by everyone is a waste of your time, the better."

What's the one piece of advice that you would give to a prospective business owner who is thinking about starting their own business for the first time?

"Do it. I mean, I'm a cliff jumper. I want everyone in the world to be a cliff jumper. I've never actually jumped off a cliff, for the record, but there's nothing like embracing risk. Seriously. My best advice is to do it. If it fails, who cares? There are hundreds of jobs out there, and there are a hundred businesses to start too. It's such a great learning experience. Just remember that if this doesn't work, there's always something else. And check your ego at the door. That will save you so much time, effort, and energy. It will allow you to focus on building your company, so you can see what it means for your family and your life."

What would you say to someone who is struggling in their business and is considering giving up?

"Take a breath. Walk away or reach out to your tribe. If you don't have a tribe, call me. I will be your people. And, don't forget that no one else will do that business the way you will."

10 STRATEGY SESSION: YOU DO NOT NEED TO KNOW IT ALL TO GET IT RIGHT

Courtney's story is a bit of a roller coaster – which is why I asked her to be one of my featured entrepreneurs for this project. It is extremely common for entrepreneurs to end up in a different business or an entirely different industry from their original starting point. If you have been in college, they tell you the academic major you graduate with will likely not be the one you declared as a freshman. The same goes for entrepreneurship. As you build businesses, you get a clearer idea of what you want to do. This isn't true of every business owner, but there's some trial and error on the path to success for most entrepreneurs. If you fall into the latter group, this chapter was written specifically for you. The concepts that follow provide an essential foundational toolset needed for every business owner with a desire for resiliency.

Entrepreneurs fancy themselves as superheroes: able to scale businesses in a single bound – and, incredibly, singlehandedly. We assume that nobody knows our business the way we do. Therefore, we need to have control over every single day-to-day facet of that business. This concept is rooted in pride. The earlier you kill that idea, the better. That mentality will destroy your sustainability. Let's break down the dangers of being a know-it-all and do-it-all.

First, this approach to managing a business is the fastest road to burnout. If you are personally drained, exhausted, and mentally fatigued, you won't be effective in your business. Self-care has become a huge buzzword, but there's some validity to the hype. You have to ensure that you create the space in your life to recharge. For entrepreneurs, that feels counterintuitive because start-up business life is supposed to be for the hardest working hustlers, right? Wrong. If you want to be in business for the long haul, establishing boundaries and processes to balance your life and your business's needs will help you grow with purpose. The sooner you can do that, the better.

Trying to take everything on yourself and relying on your own knowledge to grow your business will limit how efficiently you can build that dream. Putting your ego in check is paramount to success in business. Identifying what you do not know and finding the resources to fill in those gaps will significantly improve your chances of building a solid business that can stand the test of time. Also, by removing the need to know everything about your business, you release yourself to focus on your strengths and the facets of entrepreneurship that bring you happiness.

When you try to do and be everything in your business, you will never be caught up with your tasks. It does not matter what industry you choose; this is a universal truth. Every business requires (at a minimum) administrative tasks, accounting tasks, sales and marketing, and production management. The bigger you grow, the more time these tasks require. If these tasks don't fall in your space of experience, they take up time you should be working on growing your business. Unless you want a life of continually playing catch-up, never being able to rest, you have to learn to ask for help.

Finally, going into business with the mindset that you have it all figured out is ineffective because it leads to costly mistakes. If you're not an accountant but do your own books, you may find that your cost of pulling your taxes together at the end of the year includes twelve months of accounting corrections at a CPA's rate (which, spoiler alert, is not cheap). Building your own online store when you are technologically challenged can lead to your primary source of income breaking at the worst possible moment, leaving you at the mercy of a platform's support call line. Spare yourself the headache, heartache, and monetary cost of avoidable issues by outsourcing what you do not readily understand.

Before you can move forward in business, you have to relinquish control of things that are outside of your field of expertise. To do that, you need to be willing to check your ego at the door. To be successful in business, you don't need to know everything to get it right. You just have to know how to hire and motivate the right people to help you get it right. That may include employees, virtual assistants, consultants, or other service providers.

To start this process, you need to identify your strengths. Are you a marketing wiz? Do you have a magnetic personality that naturally draws people into whatever cause you are supporting? Are you a logistics expert? Are you a big picture visionary? Identifying who you are as an entrepreneur and the skills at which you excel will help you establish what you should spend your time doing. The rest you should consider outsourcing.

Once you've identified your strengths and the tasks that only you can do in your business, begin building your resources to create a more sustainable process for your company. There are two areas that I want you to consider when looking into outsourcing work. The first is filling the knowledge gaps that you may have. Typically, this includes accounting, regulatory compliance, marketing, and legal considerations. The second area encompasses the administrative, easy to train, time-sucking tasks that support your business's day-to-day operations. These tasks may include customer service, sales lead management, data entry, and packaging or shipping.

Courtney built her now-successful property management company because she hired an assistant to help her in areas that she was more inexperienced. Without that support, Courtney would have struggled. She may not have found her sweet spot of success. When examining her story, you can see that businesses grow more effectively with the right team running the show.

KEY TAKEAWAYS

KEY TAKEAWAYS

KEY TAKEAWAYS

11 JEFF EHLERS, ZOOM MOBILE OIL

Jeff Ehlers took a more traditional route to entrepreneurship. He holds multiple degrees and has served as a business and financial executive for numerous businesses in various industries. It makes sense that his entrepreneurial journey is as varied as the rest of his career. This is Jeff's story.

How long have you been an entrepreneur?

"Well, I'll have to do some quick math. Let's see. Probably like ten years. I've owned four businesses and was involved in the launch of two start-ups, but not as the owner."

Let's talk about the four that you've owned.

"I'll just start chronologically. The first one was an ecommerce company that sold interchangeable jelly watches. You could mix and match the colors, and it was a really hot item then. The company was made up of a group of us in college; most of us were very young, first-time entrepreneurs. We called the watches J3LL.

I also interned as an MBA student in Silicon Valley for a Financial Services firm focused on consumer debt and helping people with that debt. My niche was trying to disrupt the student loan market. Honestly, that didn't go anywhere.

Then I worked for a few startups. I was CFO and CEO for a start-up in Utah that was disrupting the 401k market. Then I started another business called Ivan Farm Technologies. That was a farm management software. I was post-college, and farming was in my background. I grew up in Eastern Idaho, working on a farm, so I was very familiar with farm agriculture. I've also had this passion and love for technology. I see all the benefits of implementing technology in a business, particularly industries that are slower to adopt, like agriculture. That business opportunity was a play to blend my two backgrounds and develop a farm management software. We had our product in beta when our largest competitor raised $5 million from venture capitalists and gave their product away for free. That crushed us. We didn't have the deep pockets to compete, and they pretty much took market share after that. But it was a good learning experience.

After Ivan Farm Technologies, I was looking around for my next opportunity, and I decided to stick with something that was more in my wheelhouse. I'm a licensed CPA with an MBA in accounting, so I decided to go to work for an accounting and CFO firm. I felt like that role played to my strengths, and I got fulfillment and enjoyment out of helping so many other businesses and companies. I've found that most business owners and company founders start their business because they are passionate about what their business does, or they are excited about a market opportunity. They aren't passionate about doing their books. But I loved helping them improve the financial health of their businesses. To help them keep tabs and useful metrics for how their business is doing was really enjoyable. Then from there came a surprise exit. When I was still building up a client base and growing and expanding my network, another company acquiring smaller independent accounting firms reached out to us. Eventually, I was rolled up that."

Let's talk about J3LL for a moment. That first time you decided to start a business, what was the pivotal moment for you that made you want to make that leap?

"It was my friend Mark. He was a great idea guy. He was one of those guys who had ideas all the time but not enough time to pursue them. He approached me with this idea and asked me if I would look into it. That was the pivotal moment; when someone I respected and trusted came to me with an opportunity. So, I checked it out, looked at the market validation, and it seemed promising."

And you guys were able to sell the product?

"We did. Yeah, we ran it for about a year. Honestly, I think there were too many 'chefs in the kitchen.' There ended up being four of us as business partners, and we started getting different visions or had different directions for where we wanted to take the company. That can be problematic because one of your advantages as a start-up or young company is that you can move fast and be nimble and hustle. You also have to adapt, but when you have that many people trying to be decision-makers and getting pulled in every direction, you lose that advantage. We ended up selling all our shares to one of the partners, and he took it and ran with it."

Is the company still in existence today?

"The partner who bought us out morphed the company into what he wanted and ended up selling the company just a few years ago. But I guess that leads to some more advice. Be careful who you're going into business with or who will be your partner. Four people are too many, and three is almost too many."

Sometimes two is too many.

"Yes. That's right. Two can sometimes be too many."

So, tell me about when you guys got your first customer at J3LL. How did that feel?

"It was awesome. We were excited! Getting that first order and seeing the payment come in made it feel real. I feel like until then, everything up to that is kind of like the saying, 'action speaks louder than words.' People can tell you all about how interested they are in your product, but you don't know for sure until someone makes that first purchase. But once you start selling your product, it gets fun."

Now that you've opened other businesses, do you still that excited feeling when you get that first customer?

"Well, there's always that element of excitement at work. I can make the analogy to sports here. It's like playing sports on a team before a game, like maybe your first game ever. You have the most jitters and nerves and are the most excited about that game. In business, you don't get that exact same feeling for every sale, but you still get excited. That's entrepreneurship. You may not get the same emotions every time, but they're still there. They're just not always at such a high-level."

Tell me how you got the word out about J3LL?

"Digital marketing, for sure. Then we made sales to try and get into retail stores, and that just takes relationship-based sales, honestly."

That was back when Facebook was just starting to ramp up, right? So how do you find that digital marketing is different now than it was when you first started?

"Back then, SEO and paid ads worked the best. It was early enough where you could still get pretty good returns on US competitive keywords if you knew what you were doing. Even today, there are still opportunities there. We were also going down the route of what we might call influencer marketing today, but it wasn't a thing back then. Then, there wasn't a term for it, but we were finding our influencers in our target space - which was basically teenagers. Then we gave them free products. Because, of course, they didn't have Instagram back then, so it was more like on Facebook and offline."

What about your subsequent ventures?

"The 401K company, that was called Benefit Guard, and it was very heavy relationship sales. Your decision-makers were small business owners with employees or financial advisors with relationships. So back then, I don't think we did digital marketing at all. It was targeted on a sales approach because we weren't going after a general consumer or a broad mass-market.

The farm software was then at such an early stage venture that the sales were mostly generated from my first and second-degree personal network connections in the agricultural industry. I think if we'd gone farther, we would have taken it to the digital space. But again, our target market, even though we were trying to sell technology to them, wasn't necessarily at the forefront of digital media.

Then with the outsourced accounting firm, we built up the business through an online marketplace, and that was great. We got vetted, and then we got listed on there, and they connected us to a lot of people looking for that kind of service."

Today, you've launched Zoom Mobile Oil – that's your current venture. What made you decide to go into the automotive industry? You've done farm technology, accounting, and now oil changes?

"I think I saw a market opportunity that I could leverage. It's not as complex as building software, and it's not as complicated as the highly regulated 401K and student loan markets. This just seemed to be an opportunity waiting. There are different phases or stages in entrepreneurship. There's an idea phase in which you see an idea or recognize one. Right? But that in and of itself is not sufficient to make the jump and take the opportunity. You have the idea, but you also need to get market validation, which is the next phase. That's where you are talking to people in the market and talking to potential customers hoping to understand them. You want to understand their pain points and understand if they are willing to pay for your idea. You need to know if there's real market value or if this isn't going to go anywhere. When doing that market validation, I discovered that the idea was promising. So that was the tipping point for getting in this space."

When you started your current business, Zoom Mobile Oil, you were already a licensed CPA with two master's degrees – which gave you a substantial background for running a business. What other tools did you learn to grow your practice?

"Well, I think one of the most valuable things from getting a formal education is the network that came out of it. Yes, the education in and of itself and the knowledge and principles you gain are definitely applicable to running a business. Having that knowledge and an understanding of how a company works and what's going on in the business world is important too. But, maybe even more importantly, or at least equally important, is the network you build. That's how I started many of these companies, or that's how I got my co-founders. I got them through the people that I met through education. Even the opportunities with Zoom came through my alumni network. These network-based opportunities helped me fill in the gaps that I need to fill in as an entrepreneur. Because you can't do everything, right? For a while, you wear all the hats just sort of out of necessity. But at some point, you need to delegate or outsource. So, having a good network in place for you to find trusted, capable people is essential.

Having mentors is critical. Mentors you view as seasoned or more experienced than you who have been through a lot in business. Because of that experience, you can turn to them for questions or advice. I think my dad is one of those mentors for me. He's been a small business owner for 25 years. Certainly, some of the people I've met in Silicon Valley have been wonderful mentors too. They've given me great perspective and insight into their experiences.

Then there is what I call 'peer support groups.' I think they are essential as well. These groups of people are going through the same things you are. Although they might not have all the answers or advice for every situation, they're perfect for emotional support and encouragement. In peer support groups, you can help each other, and I've found a lot of value in that. Having people in your life understand and empathize with what's going on is important."

There's a constant debate regarding the perceived necessity of a college education before starting a business. Do you think entrepreneurs must have a formal education?

"I think it's helpful. In general, I always recommend formal education, but maybe not necessarily as much education as I have. I might be unique and just enjoy that. I think education is valuable. You know, I think colleges are being more innovative around providing education tailored for entrepreneurs. I also believe we're going to see more innovation in the coming years as well. The University of Utah, where I got my MBA, has a new entrepreneur program. I think it's like a year and a half long, and they just teach you the basics within a class of fellow entrepreneurs. Opportunities like that are really valuable."

I know Boise State is actively promoting its venture college right now. I've seen them pull some top business talent to speak to student entrepreneurs – but I don't know that entrepreneurship itself is necessarily something that can be taught. The skills around it, however, are a different story.

"Yes. Boise State is doing a venture college. I believe colleges are starting to realize there's a demand for this type of education, and they can provide it. So yes, I generally advise getting a formal education. Sure, there's something to be said for the school of hard knocks. But I do think you can get a leg up by having a formal education.

I also think one of the things that education taught me is to be a lifelong learner. I learned how to learn, which is a really valuable skill set. I think in any job, but especially when you're an entrepreneur, you need to be a lifelong learner because you're always going to face new situations. You might get into a new industry or a new challenge, and those challenges will keep coming at you. I also advise, beyond getting a formal education, not to let learning stop there. Keep learning, keep reading books, keep following mentors, keep trying new things, and stay up to date in your industry and space."

You're in my generation – the so-called "elder millennials" – who have been on the front lines of the digital marketing revolution as professionals and entrepreneurs. It's fascinating to see how much that

landscape has changed just in the last 15 years. Do you think that many businesses go into digital marketing today thinking it's a magic, one-size-fits-all tool? And do you think that the other more traditional approaches are still relevant?

"I think part of it is that sometimes business owners can be a little slow to update our beliefs. We might be operating under the belief system of a few years ago around digital marketing. What's the right analogy? Maybe it's like mining for gold. Just a few years ago, all the gold was easy to reach and on the surface. It was all right there for the taking. But now you've got to dig a little deeper for it. Sometimes I think you can fall into the trap of believing that digital marketing is still as hot as it was a few years ago where you could easily find the gold, right?

People think that just because they put a few bucks into some ads, they're turning on the money-making machine. Maybe there was a time when that was true. But it takes a little more effort now. It takes more refinement and a strategic approach. So, I certainly think there's value in digital marketing. That's why I'm doing it, but I'm just being more strategic about it. I also think the ad platforms are also progressing and doing a better job of giving you insights into data and metrics. I believe that's important as well. Just pay attention to your analytics and adjust as needed. I think most app platforms are opening up more, or at least relative to how they were a few years ago. They're giving business owners and digital marketers more tools to help them be successful, which I appreciate."

What major roadblocks did you encounter on your journey as an entrepreneur? We talked a little bit about having too many cooks in the kitchen regarding the partnership thing. Are there any other roadblocks that stand out as far as lessons that you learn along the way?

"I think a huge one is the emotional and psychological challenges of entrepreneurship. Having been down this path and this journey for a decade or so now, it's one of the things I'd share with new entrepreneurs and maybe some experienced entrepreneurs as well. A lot of the roadblocks and challenges we face are mental. Many of the challenges are within. It's like finding your inner demons, you know, the fears, discouragement, and negative self-talk. Working through all those things, and you start to sound like a therapy session or something.

However, working through all these things is critical. If you can start conquering your inner demons, or at least mitigating them by recognizing that everybody has these fears, then you can always find the courage to press forward or advance in your business. Because everyone has those fears about taking that leap. Or everybody gets discouraged, right? You have expectations for your business or for yourself or what the market will do, but sometimes you can just get hit with things. You can have a day of highs, but within an hour, you can have some things hit you that are just like - BOOM. A huge blow. So, you have to be able to cope with these things emotionally.

I think there's a lot of benefit in getting through internal things because you are better prepared to face the external roadblocks that are coming. You feel like, 'Okay, I can get through this', or 'I'm going to learn how to get through it.' Or 'I'm going to have somebody help me as we go through this journey together.' Whether it's a peer group or a spouse, at least for me, it's essential to have some sort of emotional support there. Even the most successful entrepreneurs, and even a few billionaires I know, tell stories of just coming home and just crying. So, I think even the most successful entrepreneurs who made it huge, to the top, all experience this journey.

So, yeah, getting through it. Then you can face external things like financial challenges or trouble with a supplier or customer. I think you can then have the confidence to navigate those challenges and say, 'I'm going to figure it out. We'll get through this, and we can make it.' In the end, these psychological challenges can be for our good."

How did being an entrepreneur affect your personal life? What struggles did you experience? And what did you learn through the process? That's one of those hard points that no one likes to talk about.

"I mean, we're just human. You are a person, you know? Sometimes it's easy to compartmentalize our lives, but we're still that one person, wherever we're at. And everything kind of flows over or bleeds over, one way or the other. Your business is generally so intertwined with your life and what you're doing. So, I've personally found a few ways to cope with this. I have to put up boundaries. It's a matter of determining that you're not going to let your business impede upon some things, or at least there's going to be some break or some space. Because you still need to build healthy relationships, particularly with your family. That's been important in my life.

My advice to entrepreneurs, if you're married, is that you both need to know what you're getting into. I mean not to the same degree, of course, because a spouse is usually not going to be in the business day in and day out. But it is going to have such an influence and impact on their life. I think both of you need to understand that. I mean, you can never know what the future will bring, but it helps to understand some of the challenges you're going to face.

So, setting boundaries and having support makes all the difference. When it comes to my personal life, I found it essential to set goals personally to take care of myself. I've found I need to take time to pause and refresh. That's important, and for me, and I get that through physical exercise. There might be something different for others, but I've found exercise has other valuable benefits. I feel it helps me in my personal and business life.

As an entrepreneur, you feel this weight and pressure. It seems like it's all on you, and the only thing you can do is just to keep running. I'll think I just need to keep running with my business or keep pushing forward. You think 'I need to keep doing this', and that pressure sometimes tricks you into thinking that you need to do the work non-stop. But that's a fallacy because if you take time to sharpen the saw and take care of yourself personally, you'll be much more productive and effective with your business. You know your task list of five things to do? If you're just going non-stop, that may take you a long time to finish. But if you rest and refresh yourself, you can conquer that task list in way less time because you're more productive."

How do you handle negativity and naysayers?

"I think one of the best things I've learned is to listen to everybody, but choose who you trust. You shouldn't be blind, and you shouldn't be deaf. For instance, if market feedback is telling you something, you should listen. But in terms of decision making, I think you should listen to your inner circle of trust and people who have your best interests at heart. And when they're the ones who provide you with negative feedback or are going against what you thought, then you should learn to trust them. If it's sort of general noise, you should listen and be aware of it, but don't necessarily base decisions on their feedback. Certainly not in the same way you would if it were coming from somebody you trust. Especially since a lot of people may not understand all the circumstances of what you're doing, so they may look at things superficially and be a naysayer. Or, they may have ulterior motives. They may have something going on in their life, so their feedback is more a reflection of them than you. And when that's the case, you can be respectful and listen to their advice but only retain what is relevant to you."

What keeps you going through the hard times?

"I stay connected to the high-level vision or goal of it all. I guess the 'why' of what you're doing or the ultimate goal you're trying to achieve. Because there are so many things that end up on your plate, you can easily get caught up in the day-to-day minutia. Sure, some of that stuff you just have to do. But it can be a grind, and it can start to wear you down. So, if I keep that big picture in mind, that high-level vision, that's what keeps me going. And that's what reignites the passion sometimes. Just remembering why I wanted to do this and why I'm excited about it. That's what moves you forward. It can help keep that passion burning while you get through all the challenges and roadblocks you encounter."

Looking back. Is there anything that you would have done differently? Fewer partners?

"Yeah, that would be one. Fewer partners. There's more to that, though. It may sound like a paradox, but it's not. It's a little nuanced. Fewer partners in terms of who the business owners and decision-makers are. On the other hand, I would bring on other people in key roles when I need help, and I'd do it sooner."

So, instead of bringing on a partner, you'd hire a CMO or something.

"Yes. Exactly. I think that it's maybe a mistake of thinking you have to bring on a partner and be equal shareholders. Instead, I'd bring on people sooner to fill other roles. But I think this is often really hard to do. At least, I've observed myself and other entrepreneurs having difficulty letting go of things because it's your business. Like it's your baby. You're so used to having the ultimate accountability and responsibility for all these things, and to some degree, it's almost like a pride issue as well. But when you start to turn over some of the work, it frees you up to think about other business areas. It also allows you to thrive in areas you're good at while letting the other person thrive in areas they're good at."

What's one piece of advice you would give to a prospective business owner thinking about starting their own business?

"Do your research through low-cost experiments before you jump in. I mean, don't just judge whether an idea is good or not. Go figure it out. Let the market tell you. Figure out low-cost ways that you can test your assumptions, and you'll learn a lot that way.

For example, there is a company I knew a few years ago that wanted to purchase this specific domain name with one particular phone number before they even started the business or sold any products. This would cost

$200,000, or something like that before they even knew if people liked their products or if the business model would work. They were so focused but on the wrong things. I tried to tell them to find low-cost experiments before spending that much on a domain name. I mean, you can test these things to validate your business model without having to take on this considerable expense. So that's what I always think of in terms of a negative example. You don't want to be them, right? Before you put down $200,000 on something that you could later find out wasn't even essential, go figure out what your business is about and test those things."

What is one piece of advice you'd offer to somebody who's thinking about throwing in the towel? Maybe they've got more of an established business, and either their revenue isn't making it, or they're just burned out. Which usually it's more the latter that causes the former. What would you tell that person?

"I'd tell them that instead of making a snap decision, they should take some time to reflect. They should step back, which is hard to do when you're in that position. But whether it's for an afternoon or a day, you need to step away, process your feelings, and work through it. Then, I'd even write out things like why you got into business in the first place. Why are you even in business, and what you want in the future. I think doing that emotional processing, especially getting it out on paper, can be helpful. I mean, I can't tell you what's right or wrong in that situation. It may be different for different entrepreneurs, but I think figuring it out yourself would make an impact. Maybe you'd realize that you got out of it what you wanted, or it may be the case that it isn't what you thought it was or wanted. And then it's the right time to get out.

It's about being open to some of those outcomes and then working through it. It also goes back to having an inner trust circle that you can reach out to. They can verify that you don't have blind spots or there's something you're missing."

Any other advice?

"I'd say this idea of continual refinement or continual learning and improving is essential. We can aim for perfection. But life isn't perfect, and business isn't perfect. Reid Hoffman, the founder of LinkedIn, wrote a book called *The Start-up of You*, which is excellent. One of his principles he talks about is living your life in beta and always viewing yourself as a beta product or unfinished. Not quite there yet, or not quite perfected. I think that allows us to have a level of humility, where you want to keep learning and growing.

I think it helps keep you from becoming stale and your business from becoming stagnant.

That's why you should always have that growth mindset of just living your life in beta. And one of the things with beta is that you release a product before it's perfect. That causes you to encounter real-life situations that will refine your product and make it better. So just like with a beta product, sometimes you just have to put yourself or your business out there. Things won't be perfect yet, and you'll be a little nervous about it. But it's going to make you better."

12 STRATEGY SESSION: NAVIGATING TRENDS & OPPORTUNITIES

Jeff is another example of an entrepreneur who ended up in a completely different industry from his original business. Having worked in both direct to consumer product development and a service-based business model – he has a unique perspective. One common theme in Jeff's journey is the ability to leverage current trends and cultural shifts in his business ideas. For Jeff, that approach paid off in the majority of his ventures.

With the proliferation of the digital economy, trends, shifts, and consumer needs change faster than ever. By extension, that means those trends and shifts tend to die off more quickly than before too. While you want to meet your customers along these new buyer journey "rabbit trails,' it takes a great deal of time, effort, and money to adapt your business model or launch a new product. So how can you tell the difference between the opportunities that are worth chasing and the ones you should simply wait out?

Before we dive into the analytical process of assessing the validity of a trend or market shift, let's take a look at the psychology behind being an entrepreneur. Entrepreneurs are historically prone to "shiny object syndrome." I touched on this briefly in a previous chapter, but it is vital to understand what this phenomenon is, so you can keep it from running your life and your business into the ground.

I have a German Shepherd named Penelope. She's loyal, eager to perform well at her training tasks, and extremely passionate about taking care of her charges – namely our little family. However, despite her evident desire to be a "good dog," Penelope struggles with staying focused when a squirrel wanders into the yard, or she hears a passing car, or another dog walks by. She loses focus. She takes her eyes off of me and veers outside of her given task. Then, it takes twice as long for her to mentally engage with me and finish what she started. If I let her go off on her tangent without correction, she would completely forget what she was supposed to be doing. And, I should note, she has yet to catch that squirrel.

Entrepreneurs are in danger of operating in the same way. We want to do well in our business; it is all-consuming. And, when we see something new and shiny, we get excited and passionate about that too. The problem occurs when we allow ourselves to be so distracted by the constant revolving door of trends and consumer shifts that we lose our own stability. As a result, we never get anywhere. We never finish what we started, and we're always just trying to catch that stupid squirrel.

With Penelope, we train using artificial distractions, like chew toys, treats, and the common occurrence of my toddler running in Penelope's path during a drill. Penelope had to learn to keep her eyes on me no matter what to be successful in the task at hand. As an entrepreneur, you have to be able to train yourself to do the same thing. You have to learn to be alert and observant, but always focused on your big picture goals. Alternatively, you need to hire someone who can remind you to keep your eye on the prize and not be distracted by shiny objects.

That being said, not every trend has a limited shelf life. Some trends are indicators of a major permanent market shift. Those are the trends that require a second look. Before approaching trend-induced deviations in your business plan, consider the importance of early adaptation. If you look back on the history of American businesses, the companies that have come out of significant market changes successfully are the ones who quickly adapted to the changes. They found an innovative way to accommodate the transition in their business model and even worked to help mold the trend's direction.

As a small business owner, you may be thinking that's too much to expect from your little local store. However, digital media has empowered every business owner to make a dramatic impact on their market. But you have to be the first – or at least the first seen manipulating the trend successfully. Cultural, economic, and technological shifts are opportunities for business owners to become more competitive over time. The key is to identify which market shifts are worth chasing and which trends fit nicely into your goals.

To become a lifelong entrepreneur, to build a business that lasts more than twenty years, you must learn to perform market analysis. Not only for your industry but also for your business. The more in tune you are with your business and your market, the easier it will be to make those crucial decisions in a moment of crisis or opportunity. This book was published in 2020, which has provided substantial fodder for case studies to demonstrate the importance of this skill. As horrific as COVID-19 has been for businesses worldwide, it has also provided insight into managing dramatic shifts in local, national, and global markets.

When pandemic restrictions sent workers to a remote environment, software companies swiftly adapted to accommodate the immediate and astronomical growth opportunity. The video conferencing platform Zoom is at the forefront of this shift. When you think about it – every ad, social media post, and discussion refers to these generically as "Zoom" calls, even if your virtual meetings are held on a different platform. They became the brand most associated with virtual connectivity, and it happened nearly overnight.

It's important to note that there were dozens of options for businesses to connect virtually before the COVID-19 restrictions. GoToMeeting, Google Hangouts, Skype, Facetime, Webex, Microsoft Teams, and so on. They were all existing valid options. Yet none of them are as synonymous with virtual work as Zoom. Zoom made its debut from small software darling to publicly traded company in the spring of 2019. It's still young compared to, say, the Skype juggernaut. Zoom's user base spiked from 10 million in December 2019 to more than 200 million in March of 2020 (Haider & Rasay, 2020). Why?

Zoom had initially focused their efforts on serving businesses prior to 2020. When the shutdowns began, they shifted focus to connecting everybody for every reason. When people were reaching out to connect, Zoom was there. Some contribute this to the "network effect" – where one person invites others to use the platform. Then the new users end up using the same software after trying it on another call.

Another critical element to Zoom's success is they were incredibly diligent about managing their infrastructure. They did not wait until the surge of users to add bandwidth. As soon as those trends shifted, they jumped to accommodate them. Built on a cloud environment, Zoom is unique in that it can operate at 50% of total capacity (Evans, 2020). Compared to its competitors, this leaves it able to handle more users quickly, with fewer glitches. As business owners know, ease of use and accessibility for the consumer will always win the day.

Zoom offered a free version for general connectivity while maintaining paid versions for businesses in need of additional features. The platform became a creative center for connectivity. Breakout room features, surveys, and user tracking made it extremely attractive for event planners. The public education and university college system quickly clung to Zoom to support their classrooms because of the ease of use and bandwidth, making the platform even more domesticated.

Again, trends that take a firm hold early on typically create more trends. Privacy concerns are top of mind as remote work and video conferencing becomes normal. Considering most of their demand comes from non-paying users, this is also an example of seeing exponential success only to be met with an equally dramatic drop in revenue. What will happen when the world goes back to in-person life? Meanwhile, Microsoft is quietly adapting to the Zoom model with a beefier, end-to-end experience, so Zoom's current foothold may not be secure. Someone is already coming for Zoom's position as 'the one to beat' in the video conferencing market.

While this is a larger example than most businesses experience, it still provides a relevant lesson for every business owner. Using the COVID economy as an example, some businesses have seen an increase in profits while others struggle. For example, meal prep and delivery services, landscaping services, home repair, and game sellers all saw an increase in demand during the pandemic (Zimmerman, 2020). As a result, restaurants pivoted their business model to be strictly delivery or pickup, even selling groceries instead of prepared meals to offset costs. Whether this will be a permanent shift remains to be seen, but COVID has taught us that keeping a proverbial eye on the sky is still essential. For less extreme, more common trend projections, the formula for analysis is actually fairly straightforward.

One of the best ways to educate yourself on emerging trends is to lean on your industry association and industry trade shows. While I've warned against "shiny object syndrome," you still need to be aware of what's coming next. You just need to do so without jumping on a bandwagon before thoughtful consideration. Industry and trade associations regularly publish market research that will help you identify consumer trends year over year. These resources will save you the substantial time and energy of doing the research yourself.

Another thing to keep an eye on is cost-cutting opportunities through automation, especially when a competitor embraces such an opportunity. For example, if they can lower their margins through automation, they can charge less than you. If you think this is a possibility in your industry, you'll want to get ahead of the shift. Identifying such a move comes down to visiting your competitors' booths and websites since they will likely not share their business secrets with you.

For many small businesses, the scope is even smaller – but data is still your best friend if your goal is to build a sustainable business. If you're a local shop, you can test the data from your industry association with a little local market research. In an earlier chapter, I discussed the importance of leveraging your existing customer base by conducting surveys and tracking sales to make sure you are identifying opportunities or ways your product or service is falling short. To spot trends with this data, make sure you're storing the data year after year to ensure you can track dramatic changes quickly. If you find that a certain product or service is selling exceptionally well, or conversely, has seen a dramatic drop, you'll know more in-depth analysis is needed.

Remaining in tune with the news media is also an important indicator of market shifts. Typically, as demonstrated in the recent COVID environment, the general public reacts and adapts their buying practices based on what they see on the news or social media. As a business owner, you need to know what is happening and being said. There is no need to become obsessive about the practice, but checking in a few times a week on local and national news outlets is an important part of sensing change. To do this effectively, you need to review news and analysis from various outlets, not just the ones you prefer as an individual. Remember, this isn't about forming your own opinions. This is about reviewing the information your audience is using to make their decisions, whether you agree with it or not. Leave your personal feelings about the topic at hand at the door, and simply observe. The longer you collect data, the more you'll be able to narrow down your scope based on the sources your unique audience is reviewing. Until then, cast a wide net with an open mind.

If you're noticing a trend or opportunity once you've collected your data, having an objective and experienced business mentor look it over with you can help you analyze the situation. You'll also want to talk to your accountant and key staff members to process the information. Keep the conversation small and only include the people you trust to advise you. This kind of processing helps avoid the "shiny object" syndrome while keeping your eyes open to new opportunities and potential threats.

Armed with your data and useful advice, it's time to figure out how your business can adapt. Is there a new product you can add to your inventory to accommodate this new or changing need? Is there a new service you should offer? Do you need to reevaluate your pricing based on this data? Alternatively, is this opportunity something that requires a new or secondary business altogether? Regardless of the answer, build your plan for your new product or business. Review the quick business plan detailed in chapter eight to get you started.

Now, it's time to do a little testing. You can test the validity of your idea in a variety of ways. You can go back to that existing customer mailing list and ask them to provide feedback via a survey (i.e., "Would you purchase a product that did XYZ?"). You can expand that network by conducting a survey on social media. You can also do a soft launch to see if anyone will buy the thing.

When I decided to switch from the traditional agency model to a remote online business, one of the best pieces of advice I received was to set up a single landing page with one service package at the pricing I wanted to use. Then, promote the landing page and see if anyone bites. There is no clearer indicator of business legitimacy than having someone buy your product or service. If it works on a small scale, take what you've learned and do a full launch. This process saved me tens of thousands of dollars in missteps by bridging the information gap between what I wanted to do and what my audience needed from my business.

If your ideas prove to be valid, there is one more thing to keep in mind. This trend or opportunity may not be permanent. Having a business mentor can help you determine whether this will be a permanent shift or a temporary trend. Either way, there's no reason why you should not pursue a solid, tested business opportunity – so long as you are clear regarding the sustainability of maximizing on any given trend. If it's likely to be a short-term revenue generator, go for it. But keep your overhead as low as possible. Otherwise, there is no point in doing all of that work for very little return in the short term. If it's a permanent or long-term revenue generator, then you'll need to review sustainable growth options for this new venture. In this case, go back to Chapter Eight and Buzz's story for resources on building your plan.

KEY TAKEAWAYS

KEY TAKEAWAYS

KEY TAKEAWAYS

13 SUZIE HALL, CORNERSTONE INTERIOR DESIGN

Suzie Hall built a very successful interior design firm based in Boise, Idaho. With multiple awards and a spot on the Entrepreneur's Organization (Idaho Chapter) board, I knew Suzie would have great insight to offer entrepreneurs in all stages of business. Notably, Suzie's business, Cornerstone Interior Design, survived the 2008 recession – even in the housing and hospitality industry. This is Suzie's story.

How long have you been an entrepreneur?

"I started my journey as an entrepreneur in college, where I was in the business of editing and typing papers. Yes, this was back in the '80s when we used typewriters, and I saw a need and responded. I was as busy as I wanted to be editing and typing papers for fellow students and friends. I also managed the information center on campus. We sold food and goods, scheduled events, and a plethora of different things. I ran that for two years, so that was really a formative time for me as an entrepreneur.

After I graduated college in 1987, I worked as the sales rep for Boise Cascade office products in the Seattle area. I sold office furniture and supplies for three years and then moved to Boise in 1990. Then I worked for an office furniture dealer locally until February of 1992, and that's when I launched Cornerstone Design."

Cornerstone is your current business. Tell me about how you came up with the idea.

"In college, I wasn't sure what I wanted to do. I wasn't sure what I wanted my life and career path to be. So I decided to be a business major since I thought that would give me a broad base to start from. Still, I wasn't someone who always felt driven to build and run my own company. That wasn't ever a tangible goal in my mind.

In the first sales job, I worked on several projects with two certified interior designers. I was exposed to design there, and the passion clicked for me. I was especially inspired by the process of designing the layout and function of interior spaces while making them beautiful at the same time. I held on to that spark and excitement the four or five years I was working for other companies. Then, after I had a few years of real-world experience under my belt, my entrepreneurial spirit just bubbled up. I just realized that I wasn't able to work for anyone else. I needed to listen to that calling and go out on my own to blaze my trail."

Can you tell me more about that moment you decided to step out on your own? Was there something specific that pushed you into taking that leap and opening Cornerstone?

"I consider my journey as an entrepreneur fairly organic, gradual, and natural. It was like an awakening for me of really what I wanted to do. That was the 'aha!' moment. Finally, I could see what I wanted to do, and then the entrepreneur part of it was a natural progression for me. I was starting a family at that time, so I had an incentive to work from home and raise my family. So it all came together right in that same time frame."

Tell me about your first customer with Cornerstone.

"My first official client with Cornerstone was actually a funeral home. I don't think most people would think a funeral home would need interior design services, but I responded to the lead. I think it was published in the Idaho Business Review, or it was an RFP that went out locally. Either way, I met with the owner and had some great discussions. I built the relationship and won the project. To this day, I don't know if it was based on price. Maybe I undercut myself on price, or maybe he just really believed in me and what I was creating. That went on to be a very successful project, and I became friends with those people. It was very rewarding."

How did you get the word out about your business when you were first starting out?

"I took a broad approach. I was almost a double major in communications in college, and I've always been an extrovert. It's been easy to meet and talk to people, just getting out and networking. I was also involved in professional interior design organizations in Idaho. I say I took a broad approach, meaning that I requested and directed meetings with architects knowing that they're always looking for good interior designers to be on their team. For the most part, they were very open to meeting. And the people in Boise are very friendly.

I also asked for referrals from each client I worked with and was grateful to receive several of those early on. I joined a couple of networking groups where we met weekly to share leads and learn about what was coming up in the area. Everyone in those groups was very supportive of each other in building our businesses. There was a lot of business that came directly from that group.

I served on the board of The Interior Designers of Idaho as well. Just being in the mix with other designers and design firms helped me. I received several referrals over the years from other interior designers who didn't have the capacity for a project or didn't think they were a good fit. I think that's been important to our success as well. And all of this was before the internet, so there was a lot of hitting the pavement, getting out there, and driving.

We put up project signs at the projects that we worked at so people could see our names. I took out an ad in Idaho Statesmen one time, but I didn't receive any direct business from it. What did happen was a very good friend from high school saw that ad and reached out. So we reconnected about 16 years ago. That was Marybeth Chandler. She and Rex Chandler own Chandler Restaurants. We've become best friends, and I've done multiple projects with them on the design side, so guess it did lead to work - but it took quite a while."

You mentioned that you were a business major, so you needed extra training to get into the interior design game. Can you tell me about the steps you took to get from working in that area to running your own business? Did you have a mentor? Did you go back for additional schooling? Individual research? How did that process look for you?

"With my four or five years in office furniture sales and then launching Cornerstone, I studied for and passed the NCIDQ Examination. That is the only North American credentialing program for interior designers. About half the US states require a license to practice interior design, but Idaho is not one of them. When I sat for the exam, my work experience and my college degree qualified me to be able to sit for it.

Now, the requirements became more stringent. To sit for NCIDQ Exam, you have to have a four-year degree from a CIDA accredited college and a certain number of full-time work hours under an NCIDQ credentialed designer. That's the path if you want to be considered a professional interior designer. Since Idaho doesn't require licensing, there are a lot of people out there who call themselves designers or decorators. For me, it was vital that I achieved and operated at that highest level of professionalism because that gave the clients a guarantee that the services they receive are of the highest quality."

You started a business with a young family. Can you tell me a little bit more about that and what that experience was like for you? I know there are many women out there who see that opportunity and want to be able to work from home. Trying to get from point A to point B of making it successful is a challenge. Can you tell me a little bit more about your process?

"Well, I would say that my process was kind of a roller coaster. There would be spurts where things were very chaotic with young kids to periods where I was very focused because I knew I had to get the client work done. I wish I could say it was a gradual incline, working my way up. But with the kids and everything that comes with that, it was a roller coaster. Young kids need a lot of attention. I decided to have my kids attend preschool, and I had some good family friends who helped out. They were supportive of my journey and what I was trying to create with my business. That helped me out a lot. It gave me space to work. I knew my children were in good places where they would learn, grow, and become more well-rounded people. So that was a definite decision that I made to help balance out the chaotic nature of the early years."

Can you tell me about any major roadblocks you can remember experiencing on your journey to becoming a successful entrepreneur?

"My biggest roadblock came from getting in my own way. What I mean by that is when I started, I didn't have a big enough vision for my company. I focused too much on the small details that didn't matter in the bigger picture. Part of that is just my personal nature. I believe that part of being an entrepreneur is being aware of our personality, our personal style, and our mindset. All those things that go into making an entrepreneur can also get in our way. I thought at the time that focusing on small details would build what

I wanted and what I needed. When in reality, it became a roadblock. I needed to change my thinking, I needed to change my approach, and I needed to change my style. Especially when I started adding staff. I mean, it was kind of okay if I worked myself into a tizzy - but once I started adding staff, that wasn't fair to them."

How did you overcome that?

"It definitely didn't happen overnight. It's been a journey. I do wish I had had the label 'entrepreneur' before I started this journey. Even as a business major who graduated from a private college in 1987, the term 'entrepreneur' wasn't used. It wasn't until I joined the Entrepreneur's Organization in 2012 that I embraced the totality of being an entrepreneur. The realization hit me like a ton of bricks. It was almost like a spiritual awakening. It explained who I am and why I am the way I am.

Even today, the term continues to be significant. Just having that label has given me a tangible model for understanding myself. To understand why I'm willing to take risks, shift, change, adjust, and pivot. I believe that being an entrepreneur means that you're always curious. You're always learning, building, and growing. It's not a 40-hour workweek. It took years to learn how to balance everything.

The Entrepreneur's Organization was huge for me. I'm processing now and talking about things that I didn't normally talk about when I first joined the group. I didn't have a partner in my business. I didn't have a board. I didn't have a spouse. I didn't have anyone who really understood that entrepreneurial journey except for my Entrepreneur's Organization tribe."

How do you handle negativity or naysayers around your business both now and as you've been growing your business over the past several years?

"One of the things I've had above my desk for years is the Elaine Whiteout quote, 'Ignore people who say it can't be done.' That has always been a mantra of mine. I don't listen to naysayers. What they say doesn't affect me. My response is always like, 'Gosh, that's not how I feel.'

In the middle of the economic downturn, Cornerstone had two of the best years in our history. I believe there are a lot of reasons for that. I saw so many business owners letting that fear get to them. They just let it take over, not believing in themselves and what they had built. So many architecture firms and contractor firms closed or scaled back. I believe the mantra helped my mindset through those years because there was not a lot of positive conversation or energy shared in the universe those days."

What do you think allowed you to have such a successful few years while that was going on?

"Well, it was the mix of the work that we were doing at the time. I believe in looking at economic forecasts and keeping an eye on any upcoming workplace improvements. It might be a new technology or something like that. At the time, I was watching the economic forecast, so I made sure we had work in government, medical, commercial, multifamily, and residential. That way, all our eggs weren't in one basket.

In the residential realm, we went to the luxury market because recessions and downturns don't tend to affect those clients nearly as much as they do other clients. I was proactive in making sure our pipelines were full. Sure, a few of them fell out because of the downturn. But we still had enough going, and we had some fantastic clients during that time."

Looking back, is there anything that you would have done differently in your business?

"Of course! I would have written a business plan much earlier than I did. I also would have hired a business coach and a professional bookkeeper, both of which I have now. Both have been game-changers for me too.

I also would have been more disciplined and diligent for the first several years in setting up solid talent and processes. The interior design industry and the Treasure Valley [Idaho] are pretty small, especially when you're an independent firm like we are. Finding the right talent at the right level, with the right experience, has always been a challenge for us. Bringing on solid talent and establishing a path forward for that talent, rather than just keeping up with the projects and workload, would have made our job easier. If I could do it all again, I would have been more disciplined and diligent in doing that."

What is one piece of advice you would give people thinking about starting their own business?

"Surround yourself with only those who support and believe in you. And definitely hire a business or life coach."

What about someone who has been in business for a while and is struggling and unsure if they're going to stick it out or give up on their business? What would you tell them based on your experience?

"Reach out to a trusted mentor or advisor with a business mindset. Not a friend, family member, or somebody who is invested personally. If you don't have somebody like that, there are a lot of coaches out there who are available. I'd also tell them to make sure to share all of the details about their struggle with this person in a confidential setting. Just lay it all out there. There's power in laying it all out and talking it through with someone who has perspective. It will give you the ability to see the path forward. It will give you hope and help you see there's light at the end of the tunnel. Going through that process has helped me gain perspective. It's helped me see that you shouldn't give up."

14 STRATEGY SESSION: EMBRACE YOUR UNIQUENESS

It's lonely to be an entrepreneur. I don't mean that to downplay personal relationships with friends or family, but finding people who see the world the way you do is challenging. You always feel like you are hiding or withholding a part of yourself from the world, except when you are working on your business. Suzie has built a business that generates over $1 million in annual revenue by embracing these differences in her personality and business approach. These unique traits are found in many successful entrepreneurs and can be identified through mindset, resiliency, and just being damn good at what you do. Entrepreneurship is one field where it's good to be odd.

In my house, this phenomenon has become a bit of a joke. I even have a wall hanging in my home office that proudly announces: "A Little Weird is Good." It's something I had to come to terms with in my own self-awareness journey, and by extension, how I frame my business practices. If you are struggling in your business, taking inventory of what makes you unique is a good place to start the process of recovery.

Before we discuss defining your differentiators, we need to address another common occurrence in entrepreneurial personality types: Impostor Syndrome. Impostor Syndrome was coined in the '70s by clinical psychologists as "referring to high-achieving individuals marked by an inability to internalize their accomplishments and a persistent fear of being exposed as a 'fraud (Langford & Clance, 1993).'" Everyone experiences this at some point in their lives. Entrepreneurs tend to be achievement-focused individuals, so it makes sense that they are affected by this more than many other groups. Moreover, female entrepreneurs are statistically more likely to experience Impostor Syndrome than their male counterparts (Institute of Leadership & Management, 2011).

The business-killing facet of Impostor Syndrome is based on the way it becomes worse the better you do. The more skilled you are, the more you achieve, the stronger that sense that you are unworthy becomes. This becomes deadly to your business when you allow this feeling to keep you from adequately pricing your services or pushing forward toward progress. It's also harmful when it causes you to overcompensate by taking on too much too soon in an effort to "fake it until you make it."

The good news is Impostor Syndrome is manageable once you identify it for what it is. The process of identifying your differentiators and leveraging your uniqueness in business will help with this endeavor. Regularly revisiting this process will help to keep your focus on the reality of who you are and why your business exists, especially when those doubts start to creep back into your mind.

Before we dive into this deeper, I'd like to share a list of entrepreneurs and thought leaders who have publicly addressed their struggles with Impostor Syndrome – just to remind you that you are in excellent company.

Sheryl Sandberg (Hannon, 2014)
Maya Angelou (Warrell, 2014)
Howard Schultz (Bryant, 2010)
Barbara Corcoran (Locke, 2020)
Arianna Huffington (Giang, 2014)

Now that we've identified a critical roadblock to entrepreneurial success, we can build a plan to push through it. There are two areas you'll need to cover to adequately guard your business against the effects of entrepreneurial Impostor Syndrome. That includes your personal mindset and extends into your business brand positioning. To be successful, you have to start with your own unique qualities.

In small business leadership, what makes you different is a big part of why your employees and your customers will follow you. Starting with a review of your personal differentiators is vital to success. Maybe it's your personality – perhaps you are an outstanding public speaker or a natural influencer. Perhaps you specialize in an area of your industry that is needed but hard to find in other practitioners. Maybe your "origin story" is extraordinary.

Perhaps you win awards in your field time after time. Whatever makes you different from your peers, make a note of it.

Now, you need to go through the same practice with your business. Consider your competition and your personal differentiators, and then review the core elements of your business. How are you different? Does your product or service solve a problem that no one else can? Do you give a portion of your profits back to causes that matter in your community? How do you go the extra mile for your customers? Do you specialize in a specific part of your industry? What makes your customers happy about working with your business? Write out these differentiators.

As you work through this process, keep in mind three tests for valid business differentiators. First, is it true? While you don't want your defined differentiators to be clouded by self-doubt, you also don't want them marred by half-truths. Second, is it relevant? Remember, you want to make sure your differentiators will hold value for your audience. Third, is it provable? When considering your competitive differences in business, the more specific data you can apply to your claims, the better. In an age where anyone can say anything on the internet, consumers have become increasingly skeptical. The best way to make yourself competitive is to choose critical points you can prove with hard facts and references. Be specific and have the data to back up your claims.

For example, a weak business differentiator would be "We are committed to excellent customer service." By contrast, a strong differentiator would be, "We have more than 300 five-star Google reviews from happy customers!" This statement powerfully demonstrates that you care about your customers. It's also easy for your audience to verify.

Now that you've clearly defined what sets you apart, you can use the information to revisit your existing business plan and practices. What isn't matching your differentiators? What can be improved, reframed, or removed from your business approach? Is your marketing message using your differentiators properly? Is there a better way to present your brand to your audience? Is there a cause you should be supporting that would amplify your unique approach to doing business? Are your employees clear on what makes your business different? If not, spend some time on training and fostering buy-in.

Remember, finding success as an entrepreneur means that you created something different from the norm. That's a good thing. When you begin to doubt yourself or your ability to be competitive in business, revisit the things that set you apart from the crowd. That clarity will not remain unless you are consistent in feeding the narrative that what makes you different makes you better.

Above all, never be afraid to be a little weird – the world needs it.

KEY TAKEAWAYS

KEY TAKEAWAYS

KEY TAKEAWAYS

15 ANDREW OWCZARECK, BUSINESS MENTOR

When I started interviewing for this book, Andrew Owczarek – or Andy O. as I know him – was one of the first people I wanted to include. Andy has worked in multiple facets of business ownership and management. Today, he serves as a business investor and a mentor with Treasure Valley SCORE in Idaho. Andy provides a unique insight for businesses looking for investor funding. This is Andy's story.

Tell me about your history as an entrepreneur.

"Let's start with serendipity and luck. Because to some extent, serendipity and luck have everything to do with things - particularly when you're young and don't have a specific life direction. I did not have a particular life direction that my mother or father pointed me in. They didn't say, 'Go be a lawyer or a doctor,' or anything else like that. All they wanted me to do was to be good at school. As serendipity would have it, I was lucky to have some technical skills. By that, I meant that I was particularly good at physics, science, and math. That set me up for further serendipity when I went into the Air Force. The Air Force decided to put me in a technical position, which then exposed me to lots of technical people, some of whom were doing interesting, exciting, and productive things.

I started out by having a reasonable education then being lucky enough to be put in a place where pieces of that education helped me with other people that I meet. Specifically, I met people with technical backgrounds who were starting businesses at the time. Being young, naïve, and stupid, I said, 'This looks like fun.' I had no business experience at that point in time. All I had was technical knowledge and some amount of curiosity. Then I was exposed to people who had similar backgrounds and instincts. Except they had it for three, five, ten, and fifteen years. I found it to be a fun and interesting experience. It started out with 'How can I play in the sandbox?' because the sandbox looked fun.

From there, what happened is what happens to many people who start businesses. In conversations with some of my acquaintances, we identified a product or products that we said we would like to have but didn't exist in the marketplace. We thought to ourselves, being relatively ignorant, 'Since we have the technical skills, why don't we design and build this product?' Then we'd have it for ourselves. This was in the era before market research was very sophisticated. We thought, 'Surely if we want it, there must be a lot of people out there like us who want it too, right?' That's how we got started. We had a couple of engineers, and I ended up being a salesman and operations manager. We identified a product that we all personally wanted to have, and we said, 'Let's build this sucker.'

We didn't know how to price it, so we had to figure that out. We didn't know what demand might or might not be, so we had to try and figure out how to sell it. At that point in time, when we were doing this, we were all working basically for nothing. We borrowed money from friends and family. Way back when, going back to 1971, we managed to assemble $150,000. In today's money would be real money. We ended up getting a loan from a bank because a number of us were gainfully employed. We put in $150,000, started a business, and we started building stuff. That was before China. Before cheap manufacturing overseas. We ended up building stuff in a lab outside of Boston.

Then the reality dawned on us that we built a wonderful product that we were happy with, but we didn't know either how to tap into or create demand in the marketplace. Over the course of the next two and a half years, the product died. If you can't generate sales, things kind of fade into the sunset. And we weren't any good at that. I couldn't even tell you at this point, in retrospect, if we had priced it right because we didn't know what we needed to price it at. We may have overpriced it because we were ignorant. But the fact of the matter is, the first entrepreneurial venture into the world, which started by building a product that we thought we needed, went away.

It was a fantastic learning experience. We didn't know what we didn't know - but over time, we figured it out. The good news was when we closed up shop on the business, we didn't owe the bank anything. We all collectively lost our initial investment and investments from friends and people who put money in. That, eventually, over three years went to zero. It was a massive learning curve that set the stage for the future for some of us. At least three of us went on to create and build separate, additional businesses on the ashes of that experience."

How many businesses have you owned or managed over the course of your career?

"About three dozen."

Are they all in the STEM industry?

"They're in all kinds of different industries; manufacturing, service, retail, all kinds. I still manage four businesses today in different industries: construction, retailing, service, and manufacturing. I have one in each currently."

What would you consider your most successful business?

"There is some semblance of trends between what I started doing when I was young and where I've ended up. I got exposed in my career after the first meltdown managing several small businesses for a large company. There I learned what to do and what not to do using somebody else's money. At the time, I was exposed to various things: logistics, running trucks, warehouses, services, beauty salons, restaurants, you name it.

Over the last 15 or 20 years, I've had two very successful businesses. One was in retailing, and the other in the service business. Both do impressive numbers for the markets that they're in and make terrific profits. Both of them are amenable to fine-tuning, whereas the other two businesses I currently run, in manufacturing and construction, are limited by what you can do well. Those companies are doing well too, but they're also not if you had to rank based on profitability as a percentage or market share. The retailer and the service business would be far and away the strongest enterprises I've been associated with.

Ultimately, all of the owners who started with relatively small capitalization have seen their net worth go into the millions because of doing what they're doing exceptionally well in their niches and marketplaces. I'm particularly enthused and proud of that. Along the way, with that, of course, I've made a little bit of money."

As far as your business education goes, do you have a formal degree? Or was it the technical skills you picked up when you went into the Air Force that you built from?

"I'd say it was street skills, and then I built from there. I also had another serendipitous event. After the first business meltdown, I went to work for what was then called Federated Department Stores. Federated Department Stores was an interesting entity in that it had divisions across the country that operated fairly autonomously. In each region, the divisions had slightly different market positions. They each had their own presidents and chairmen who were supposed to run their businesses as if they were their own businesses. The headquarters in Cincinnati was pretty much a financial entity, a bank. That experience was very valuable to me as a next step in education.

Federated essentially had many businesses under their roof, but every month they published the financial results from all divisions to every other division in the country. So, for example, if you were sitting in Dallas and running the warehouse, you could look at the warehouse numbers for divisions across the country and compare yourself against them. You could go to school on them. The company's culture was one where people were expected to talk to one another and help each other improve month-in, month-out, year-in, and year-out. The goal was to share best practices. Over time, that meant the whole enterprise got better. Through that experience, I learned how to dissect what the most successful divisions were doing and then implement those strategies too.

The ten years that I spent running different businesses for the Federation is where I got most of my schooling. It was practical schooling because you looked at results and asked people, 'What are you doing differently? Why is this working for you better than it's working for somebody else?' The numbers tell a compelling story. You get rated internally in the company by how well you're doing and how well you rank on the numbers compared to other people. It was just like dealing in the free marketplace. You had a ready set of comparisons. You had a way to see if you were doing well or poorly. We had market information from across the country by category and by business. I learned that it was a useful way to look at things. I was able to take that skill set to other companies. I could use that methodology to get information and then copy, emulate, and adjust what I was doing to get the best results."

For the other businesses that you've done, has it been you taking out a start-up, or have you operated more as an investor manager?

"Most have been in the capacity of investor manager after the initial three years. After that initial wave, it's all been people coming to me with opportunities. I've never been part of an angel group or anything else like that. It's been word of mouth. People who have been successful working with me tell other people who are looking to grow and build."

What do you look for when you're looking at investing in a company?

"It's going to sound very egotistical, but it's, 'Can I make a sufficient difference to make the risk of investment of time and money worthwhile?' I'd like to tell you that there's a spreadsheet where you examine the criteria, but it's more of a gut instinct after all of these years. I can look at the operating results of a business and do some homework on similar or related businesses to decide whether I see an opportunity. I also consider the timeframe for building, advancing, or expanding. Usually, almost all of these enterprises are three to five-year activities.

I also look at management and ownership because I've had cases where I've identified things, but couldn't make the management team or other investors listen sufficiently to make it worthwhile. In other words, there's no shortage of opportunities. It's a filtering process based on what my gut says the risk and upside over two, three, four, or five years is. People you don't think you can work with or don't listen are part of that risk. I have been down the road with some that have gone nowhere. Then what you do is find amicable separations.

I learned a long time ago that you document and agree on how you're going to work together before you exchange any money. That makes the separation process considerably more manageable if you've identified and put those things in place before you've gotten involved. The same goes for my volunteer mentoring with SCORE. When people come into SCORE with partnerships, family relationships, and so forth, one of the first things I encourage them to do is make sure they have a written agreement for how it's all going to work before they go further down the road.

Most of the lessons I've learned have been common sense, practical, in the trenches kinds of things. Do your homework and due diligence on the business. Look for opportunities, and if you find them and start engaging in a conversation, document everything in writing before any significant amount of money changes hands. Then do versions of the proverbial business plan. If you go back to my life and listen to back to the physics, math background, and first experiences - it's easy to see why I would tend to, in business, be more structured and less spontaneous."

Considering you've worked in multiple industries, can you tell me

how current technology, mainly the internet, has changed how you approach doing business?

"My answer primarily highlights a change in the retail space, but it still applies across the board to many industries. It just happens to be easier to quantify in retailing. A professor at NYU or somewhere in New York studied retailing and pricing. He studied the amount of time that a product spent at its first asking price. In 2008-2010, it was approximately four to six months. In 2016 and 2017, his analysis showed that products spent one to three months at the first asking price. Then, they went through a succession of markdowns until, ultimately, the retailer got rid of what was left. I analyzed that, and what it showed was - all things being equal - the rapid price changes resulted in a seven percent lower margin for the retailer. Because the price changes happen faster, they sold less stuff at a higher price because it wasn't out there for so long.

I'll give you a specific example. Let's say you were selling shoes before the days of e-commerce. If you bought a yellow shoe in size 10 and put it out on the floor in your store, it might be there for three months before you figured out that you weren't going to sell that shoe in the quantities you bought. Simply because the only information you had on the marketplace was from the customers who came into your store. In today's world, there may be 300 people selling yellow sneakers in size 10, and because people shop online and have the ability to compare, you know much faster now whether or not you'll be able to sell those 10 pairs of yellow sneakers. You will know in a couple of weeks, and you can shop competitors to see what they're doing. You can take action more rapidly to deal with your problems, but then that puts pressure on you to be efficient in the back of the house because you're getting less margin on the front side.

The pricing of products has gotten more competitive, and the free exchange of information ensures everyone has access to the same pricing information. It's a much larger arena and much larger sandbox that you play in these days, and you have to be aware of what's in the sandbox.

Another typical comparison that I use is, ten years ago, 'marketing' was putting an ad in the yellow pages. If you place an ad in the yellow pages for those size ten yellow sneakers, your competitor would do the same. But the exposure of that information was relatively thin. It was your local market, or wherever the yellow pages went, that had access to it. Now your exposure and competitiveness - whether it's for services or products - is global, or at least mega-regional. You can't afford to be wrong. That tends to bring prices down to the lowest common denominator in terms of what customers are willing to pay for a given product or service.

As a retailer, you now have to be sharper on your pricing. You have to be faster in reacting to prices that are too high or wrong in the marketplace. Think about airline tickets. Airline tickets are now demand priced because their sales are going through the internet, and people can instantaneously compare the cost of flying from Denver to New York - easily and instantaneously. There are software packages that do it for you. You can go to Expedia or whatever it happens to be. No longer do you set the price and sell in a vacuum - waiting for the results over a longer period - only to figure out that you made a mistake and were inefficient. You get efficient much faster these days.

On top of that is the whole 'brouhaha' about personal information and being able to market selectively. You can now identify who's going to buy those size 10 yellow sneakers because you know who buys yellow sleeping bags. You can also market more selectively because you have customer demographic and habit information that we never had before.

We just went through an exercise with SCORE. We had a mailing list of 4400 people. That mailing list included no characteristics of customers. So we identified three categories of services and sent them to people with a note saying, 'Would you like to continue to get information on these three things: workshops, newsletters, or something else?' We took our 4400 unqualified customers down to a list of 450 people who confirmed they wanted information on that service. That's a massive change in terms of the business marketplace, selling things, and being efficient."

Looking back, can you remember some of the more prolific roadblocks that either you've helped business owners overcome or that you've overcome as a business owner yourself? And how were you able to navigate those?

"Sure. A specific roadblock, which I'm loath to highlight to people starting just out, is understanding financial reports like spreadsheets, balance sheets, and profit and loss reports. There's a whole bunch of things that go into running a business, like pricing and margin. That was a huge roadblock for me. I knew nothing about any of that when I got started. Until I could go to class, teach myself, and learn bits and pieces of that, I would say I had a huge wall to climb in terms of being successful. Unless you understand the bits and pieces, and the specific ramifications for a given business, it's hard to make the right kind of business investment and operational decisions. You have to know where each decision is going to lead, and you have to be able to do scenarios, spreadsheets, and things like that. That was a huge roadblock that I had to get past."

What are some tips and strategies you offer businesses you mentor or businesses that you've run yourself for marketing and getting the word out about the business on a smaller budget?

"First of all, have a budget. Then track the effectiveness of your tactics within that budget. People used to use their marketing analysis, if they had any at all, with couponing. That was how they would track whether or not an offer made sense to a customer. I have always tried to get people to find ways for their businesses to determine whether a particular marketing activity brought any return. As you determine activities are effective, you do more of them. When activities are ineffective, you do less of them.'

The internet has made the tracking of marketing effectiveness - particularly in terms of social media, web pages, and electronic offers - a whole new ball game. We use these newer strategies the way we used to use coupons. Except coupons were always hard to keep track of. They'd get lost, and you had to depend on codes and offers through point-of-sales systems. Or through salespeople, if you were selling wholesale. The tracking of offers and results in marketing programs have gotten better and easier. I always encourage people, outside of a base core budget for brand identity - which means stationery, a logo, and that kind of thing - that what you should do trackable activities that allow you to quantify results if at all possible."

What's one piece of advice you'd give to somebody looking to start their own business?

"Do your homework on the market and similar businesses. Get educated on what makes those businesses successful or unsuccessful. Then identify how you're going to be different and better. Where possible, do some market research to see if other people are going to operate the way you will.

Our market research on our first company was lacking. We built an excellent product, but we didn't know that tens of thousands of other people wanted to do the same thing. We didn't do our homework. We didn't investigate whether or not what we were trying to do was viable or if anybody was doing something similar that made sense in the marketplace. My advice is to do some homework on related or similar businesses to determine whether or not what you're trying to do has merit. In the end, you have to figure out how you're going to be different."

What about somebody who has been in business for a while and they're getting to that point where they're burned out and thinking about giving up on the business. What would you tell them?

"That's hard. Once you lose the soul for it, you need to get out of Dodge. What happens is the business erodes inch, by inch, by inch. It usually doesn't happen in miles. You slowly stop doing the things that you used to do to make the business successful. All of a sudden, you wake up, and you're just trying to keep up with having enough money in the bank to survive. Once you get to that point that you can't sustain that energy level or drive, get out. Find someone else to give the business to. Find someone to turn it over to. Sell it and do something else.

The worst thing you can do is be in a lousy mood and not want to come to work. You'll stop doing the things that are necessary to make the business successful. I've been through a considerable number of generational transitions and changes of ownership due to retirement. Changes in attitude and so forth are challenging, but the alternative is worse. You have to commit to saying, 'Once I'm no longer married to this, I have to find something else to do or a different way to do it' and hope over time that you've been successful enough that you don't have financial handcuffs.

I've seen that happen. We've had people in SCORE who've run family businesses for an extended period of time. They were burned out, and the companies had essentially no market value. Because they got bad advice along the way, they didn't have property or something else to fall back on. They had gotten poor advice and spent all of the money they had made, expecting that they would go on forever as they were. But they should have been looking out over the horizon and planning, so they had something to fall back on when they get to the point of wanting to get out of it all. That's the kind of advice that I give folks who have been in business for a while but never looked towards the far end of the trail."

What about somebody who has built a successful business – whatever that looks like in their industry – and they're looking at exit strategies. What would you recommend for them to begin that process?

"Long before you're ready for the exit strategy, you have to figure out what the exit strategy for your particular business is. Some businesses are flat out not sellable. There's no market for them. No one's going to buy them. You've got to decide what the possible exit strategies for your business are. If the company is not sellable, you have to look at the assets that will be left when you're ready to close the business. Can you liquidate them? You need to plan early for how you're going to relieve yourself of that business.

There's one SCORE client that I've worked with who has facilities and inventory. The facilities have ongoing value having nothing to do with his business. They're just plain real estate assets. If he needs to, he can have a fire sale on the inventory to liquidate the business and collect a nice rent check on the property. Or he can sell the property for what it's worth because he's not selling the business.

I have another gentleman I've worked with who has a sellable business, theoretically, but likely only because he is unique in approaching and managing the business. He's got a unique skill set. I'm encouraging him to build up the assets other than the value of the business because the value of the business is him. And no one is going to pay him what that is worth when he's no longer involved with it, so he's got to have assets elsewhere because he probably will have to liquidate the business. And then, if he's lucky, he'll be able to sell it for assets.

Another guy I worked with did the same thing. He didn't own the building. He didn't own the facility. He spent all of the money he made over time, thinking that he could sell the business for three million dollars or some other large number when he wanted to be done. In the end, that was just not realistic. And he's stuck. He has to keep working.

I've had three or four people different people come through SCORE who had all taken the money out of their business and spent it. When it came time for them to get exit the business, they had no other source of income. They were stuck. That's why you've got to identify your exit strategy early on and put things in place to maximize the likelihood that the business will end up the way you want it."

Is there anything else that we haven't covered?

"If you do your homework and you're willing to work hard, it's easier to look past the naysayers because you have a much larger chance of success. In that case, you don't have to worry about them. You should worry about naysayers if you're not willing to work as hard as it takes or if you've got no value proposition or strategy to carry you along.

What keeps you going through hard times is the confidence that you're going to come out of it. Hard times come and go, and it's just having confidence that you're doing the right thing. You're not riding a bubble; you're riding something solid. There may be a little bit less air in that tire, but you're going to make it through because you're doing the right things. You're going to be a survivor. I don't know any way to identify confidence in business better than that."

16 STRATEGY SESSION: MAXIMIZE YOUR MENTOR RELATIONSHIPS

Throughout this book, there's a recurring theme, and that's the importance of finding an objective third party who can be a sounding board for the big decisions in your business. Those people are mentors. For me, there are few people I trust in this role more than Andrew Owczarek. While he's never been my formal mentor, I have referred to his advice many times throughout my entrepreneurial career. I've also co-mentored business owners with Andy through my time at our local SCORE chapter. He is a wealth of information, and I knew his insight would be invaluable for business owners struggling to navigate the current climate.

As much as I would love for this book to be a cure-all for all of your business ills, it's simply not possible. Every business is different, every entrepreneur has different strengths, and the market will ebb and flow over time. So, the best piece of advice I can give you is to find an experienced mentor to help you fill in the gaps. You need that one-on-one connection to work through problems objectively.

The idea of finding a mentor is not a new concept for many entrepreneurs. However, I have found that most business owners are at a loss on finding and building a beneficial relationship with the right person. Since this is such a vital part of business success, I want to dedicate an entire chapter to breaking down the best way to approach this process. After all, as Carson Gracie once said: "If you want to be a lion, you must train with lions."

Foundations of an Effective Mentor-Mentee Relationship

Like any relationship, mentor relationships require honesty and a lot of work. Otherwise, they remain surface-level – which is a waste of time for both you and your mentor. You need to consider the background and personality type of your ideal mentor. You'll also need to be okay with them seeing the rougher sides of your business. This needs to be a relationship of trust. Here's what you need to build a successful mentor-mentee relationship.

The first thing you need to do is check your ego at the door. I've mentioned this multiple times already, and I'm likely to do it again. If you want to humble yourself, open a business. Because the only way you will be successful is to recognize that you cannot do or know it all, and you need help. When you're a super competitive, Type-A, entrepreneurial type – this is a tall order. Before you begin to look for a mentor, you need to be in the headspace of accepting criticism. Your mentor's role is to help you identify potential risk factors and offer insight on how to mitigate those risks. If you're not willing to keep an open mind, it's not a worthwhile exercise.

The second thing you need to consider is finding someone in your current industry. This point may sound obvious, but you could find a great mentor who doesn't know your industry. Going that route can be problematic for obvious reasons. You want someone who can speak to your market, processes, and regulatory compliance issues. These vary significantly by industry – and you want a mentor who is knowledgeable in the best practices for your unique business. The caveat to this is the understanding that many standard business processes are relatively universal. So, it is possible to have a worthwhile mentor relationship with someone outside of your industry. If you find that you resonate with a more experienced business owner in a different field, you can always take the approach of having multiple mentors for different needs. Just make sure you keep looking for that industry-specific expert.

Another core component of a successful mentor-mentee relationship is honesty. Your mentor can only provide apt advice for your business if they fully understand the situation. You do yourself no service by hiding the less-than-perfect aspects of your business. If you're struggling with cash flow, be honest about your spending habits. If you're struggling with employee management, be honest about your role in the issues thus far. This is where building trust is so important.

You want to find a mentor who is okay with being goal-driven. If you just aimlessly meet for coffee now and again – you're likely to spend most of the time gabbing about things of little consequence. Such an arrangement won't serve either of you. Find a mentor who is experienced with and willing to help you with set goals. Maybe that means tackling cash flow in the first quarter, hammering out a new business plan in the next, or whatever your needs are at the time. Use the SMART goal method – your goals should be **S**pecific, **M**easurable, **A**chievable, **R**elevant, and **T**ime-bound.

Finally, mentoring relationships should never be a one-way street. Find a way to help your mentor as a "thank you" for their time. Perhaps that means helping them learn new technology, establish a new process improvement, or even introducing them into your network. After all, this business life always leaves room for something new to learn. Don't make the mentor/mentee relationship all about what you can get, but also what you can give. That mutual respect and understanding will help both of you long after the relationship runs its course.

Finding the Right Mentor

Now that you know what it takes to build a worthwhile mentor-mentee relationship, you have a better understanding of the importance of finding the right mentor. There are a few different ways to go about sourcing a mentor. The best option for you relies on your network's size and quality and how quickly you need the support. This is where you start.

If you're not in a rush to find a mentor, you may find some quality candidates in your existing network. This option can provide a large subsection of fellow business owners, but it can also be intimidating. It's not like you can invite someone randomly for coffee and ask them to be a mentor. The progression from network contact to mentor is one that takes months or years to develop organically. Also, it's up to the two of you to get there. If you have someone who is familiar with you and has more than a surface-level interest in your goals – you may be in a position to ask sooner rather than later.

If that whole paragraph left you feeling overwhelmed or need support right away – there is another option. You can visit your local Small Business Administration (SBA), Small Business Development Center (SBDC), or SCORE office to be paired with a mentor. The benefit of these sorts of programs is that they have a time-tested formula to pair you with the right person and build the relationship. It is all spelled out for you. All of the foundational pillars of business mentor relationships still apply, but you will be operating within a more controlled environment. This removes a great deal of the intimidation factor, which is useful if this is your first foray into mentor relationships.

When to Find a New Mentor

So what happens when you've found a mentor, but the relationship is no longer rewarding? Perhaps it is a new relationship, and your personalities don't mesh. Alternatively, it may be a long-standing relationship that has run its course – meaning you are no longer growing with your mentor. If things just aren't moving forward, regardless of why, you may want to find a new mentor. This is where honesty comes into play again. If you have a goal with your mentor and, for whatever reason, you cannot complete that goal – it's time to have an open discussion about why.

If you find that things just aren't working out with your current mentor, all of that effort doesn't go to waste. If your mentor has been with you for a decent amount of time with a mostly positive experience, you don't just want to cast that relationship aside. Instead, scale it back to a colleague relationship. That network contact is still valuable, and it's always a good idea to keep fellow business owners who understand you in your social circle.

If you're working with a SCORE, SBA, or SBDC mentor – the good news is the same organization can likely find you a mentor who will better fit your needs. Hopefully, you've grown your network by this time as well. That leaves the door open for an organic mentor-mentee to develop. If you're fortunate, by the time you've 'outgrown' your existing mentor, you already have someone in your sphere who can fill the role more effectively for your next stage of business.

The Difference Between a Mentor and a Coach

One more key item I need to cover before sending you down the road of finding the perfect mentor is the difference between a mentor and a coach. I have heard these terms used interchangeably many times, and I cringe at each occurrence. When I say, "Find a mentor," I do not want you to run out and hire that one coach you know from your favorite networking group. Both roles can be useful, and there is some overlap – but there are significant differences that you need to consider before you engage someone in either position.

A mentor relationship is, first and foremost, not a paid engagement in most cases. Coaches tend to be fee-based, either by the hour or on a program package rate. Coaches typically have created a set program for each of their clients that is proprietary to them or the company they work for. It is their job to essentially assess, instruct, and monitor you within that program's timeframe. On the other hand, mentors provide a two-way discussion based on personal experience and insight from operating a business in your industry or market. They can help you manage smaller projects, but they are best used for the big picture conversations like strategic growth and scalability.

The most significant difference between the two practices is that coaching is more transactional and task-oriented, while mentoring is relationship-oriented. A coach will walk you through a structured process of reviewing specific topics and creating the tasks for you to address. They may even have an accountability component to their program, but the overall engagement is typically limited to a certain amount of time. By contrast, a mentor is much more expansive in their scope of pulling your potential out of you. The relationship may last years in this endeavor. The goals and scope will change throughout that time, and you should be contributing as much as you gain from the other party.

As you've heard in interviews throughout this book, both mentors and coaches can add significant value to your business when carefully sourced and utilized correctly. If you are reading this book, there is a good chance you are either a brand new business owner, or you are struggling. You need the big picture vision first before you can be successful in building your processes. Seek out your experienced mentor and build that relationship as soon as you can. Then, if you find that you need more hands-on assistance in a specific area, you can add a quality coach to your team.

KEY TAKEAWAYS

KEY TAKEAWAYS

KEY TAKEAWAYS

17 BRANDON WRIGHT, DILLON PLUMBING

Brandon Wright is a unique entrepreneur. He has a reputation for being a leader in his networking circuit. He is one of those people who seems like an endless resource of "who's who" for whatever services your business needs. While being a thought leader in the Idaho business community, Brandon has managed to build and sell one business, then buy and grow another. This is Brandon's story.

How long have you been an entrepreneur?

"It started in 1999 with UltraClean Carpet & Upholstery Cleaning. I worked in that industry for a year for somebody else. Then one of my customers came up to me and said, 'You're pretty good at this. You're the only one that I like cleaning my carpets. You should start up your own business.' I had never even thought about it. But the fact that somebody believed in me and saw my potential sparked up a little inspiration in me. It led me to think that maybe I should start a business.

On January 1st of 1999, I gave my two weeks' notice at my job. After that, I went to the bank and asked for financing. I told them I wanted to start up my own business. Of course, every banker had a smile on their face and said they could help me with that. But I had no credit. I had no income either. I had just gotten my last paycheck of $416, so they said, 'Nope. Sorry. Declined.' I ended up going to eight different banks. Every single one promised to help me, and then none of them did.

Just as I was about to give up, because I really couldn't think of any other way to get the equipment I needed, our supplier at the carpet cleaning store approached me with an opportunity. He said, 'I know somebody that started up a business two months ago, and they don't want to do it. Maybe you can take over their payments.' They had payments on a personal loan, so I took on that debt. Of course, being young, I had a high-interest loan, and it was a short note, too. It was a two-year, maybe three-year note. I bought an old van without power steering, a portable carpet cleaner, and a short customer list that turned out to be made up of the previous owner's friends. That's how I started my business.

The thing is, I didn't even have enough money to buy chemicals. I had to ask my supplier for free samples. Then I would do a job with the samples he gave me and use the money I made to buy chemicals for the next job. Eventually, we started making enough money to buy chemicals and other supplies regularly.

At the same time, we hit the slowest time of the year for carpet cleaning. Nobody had their carpets cleaned in January, February, or March. So right after I got the equipment, I sat around waiting for the phone to ring. I had a list of ten people who had indicated to me they wanted their carpets cleaned in January. When I called to book the appointments, each of them said the same things: 'Oh, we spent too much money for Christmas' or 'The weather isn't good.' None of the clients I thought I had panned out. I didn't get a single phone call for two weeks. My phone didn't ring once in two weeks.

Being young like that, I mistakenly thought that the phone was going to ring just because I was in business. But it didn't. I knew I would have to pay rent in two weeks, so I got a job delivering pizza to get by. That helped me pay rent, but it also turned into a great marketing strategy."

And you sold UltraClean in 2016?

"Yes. Two weeks shy of 18 years in business."

And then you purchased your current business, Dillon Plumbing?

"Yes. In January of 2018."

And in the meantime, you were running a podcast/radio show on Wright Stuff Radio and Wright Stuff Media? And you wrote three books in that period as well?

"That's right."

With UltraClean, was there any reason you went into upholstery, cleaning, and restoration, or was it just an opportunity you decided to run with?

"If you take a look at my business career, UltraClean was the business in which I learned everything. With Dillon Plumbing, I could execute everything I learned. For that reason, Dillon Plumbing has been successful a lot faster. I've been able to move quicker and more efficiently to achieve the growth that we've had. Like many new entrepreneurs, I started with UltraClean because I was already in the trade. I knew the trade and felt comfortable with it since I started in it as a technician.

I fell into UltraClean, and I did Dillon on purpose. But the one similarity between the two is that I got key people in place early. When I first started UltraClean, I had a bookkeeper named Joan. Joan previously worked as a bookkeeper for a large restoration company in California. She could work part-time, and one of the big things about her is that she controlled my finances. If you take managing finances away from a business owner's responsibilities, their only job is to serve customers and make money. I was fortunate for the first two years to have her do that. To have someone that I trusted. I firmly believe that I wouldn't have made it in business if I did not have her. I just didn't have the financial mentality or the acuteness and maturity to run a business. She was a big part of the success of the business."

How did you figure out the steps to grow UltraClean? Did you have a business mentor that you relied on? Was it just trial and error? Did you figure things out along the way?

"I didn't purposefully grow UltraClean. UltraClean grew because of who I am. With almost every small business, people choose that company because they know, like, or trust the owner. In the trade business, that is how most companies get to a certain point or level of growth.

My first marketing strategy was tied to my job at the pizza place. I thought, 'I'm delivering 30-40 pizzas every night, so how do I make these people potential customers for a carpet cleaning company without crossing an ethical boundary?' I did that by putting a magnet on my car. I'd ring the doorbell and stand at the side of the door. When they open up the door, the first thing they see is my car, and they'd say, 'Carpet cleaning?' I'd say, 'No, no. I got your pizza. But since you asked, here's a coupon or a business card.'

When I wasn't delivering pizza, but was in the restaurant serving customers, I had conversations with people. Customer service is about conversations, and the customers would ask what I did outside of that job. When I explained, someone would ultimately tell me they needed carpet cleaning. It was easy to find business. I met property managers and different types of customers through the pizza job, so it was easy to get business from them. That's how you start building those relationships and growing the business."

Tell me about your first paying customer that you got with UltraClean. Can you tell me about that experience and how it felt to earn that first dollar?

"I don't know exactly who my first customer was, but I believe it was Paisano's Italian Restaurant in downtown Meridian. I remember using the free samples in a pump sprayer. A carpet cleaner uses everything automated, but I had a pump sprayer. I had to pump all my chemicals. I remember that first job was $150. That allowed me to buy a gallon of preconditioner. I remember getting that $150 and thinking, 'Wow. That is good money.' A year down the road, or even today, if I were to get that job, it'd probably be a $600 job. But for me, $150 was a lot of money. And being an Italian restaurant with lots of grease, it took a lot of time. But they were happy with the work. Not to mention, the owners became great friends. That was over 20 years ago, and I'm still friends with the granddaughters of the owner. That's incredible. It tells you how powerful relationships can be, especially when they start as a customer."

Tell me about the more notable roadblocks that you experienced along the way and how you overcame them.

"When I look at roadblocks, I categorize them in three different ways: finances, people, and liabilities. I experienced a liability roadblock went I went from carpet cleaning to the restoration industry. In restoration, you deal with water damage and mold. That work is exceptionally high risk. For 18 years, I made it without a lawsuit. It wasn't until after I sold the business that I got served my first lawsuit. Luckily, we were not at fault, and it was eventually dropped. But it was the first lawsuit.

I'm also dealing with my first lawsuit at Dillon Plumbing. To go that long without a lawsuit in a service business is pretty incredible. I think that can be attributed to taking care of problems right away when you screw up. You have to make sure you own your part, and sometimes, you have to own things that aren't yours because you don't want them to escalate. That's a massive part of business that I think a lot of business owners don't get.

The second part is people. In 2005, I was making about $1.7 million in annual revenue. I realized that I had 26 employees and was broke. I was making $50,000 a year, which is less than a lot of my employees made. When I took my total revenue and paid my employees, I was left with something like $50,000. I just remember thinking, 'We're not making money.' I didn't have the financial maturity at that point to know what I was looking at, but I knew we weren't making it. I also knew things weren't going to change because we kept having production issues, customer service issues, quality issues, and we weren't making money. Everything was wrong. That's when I realized we had to start running it as a business. About a year later, we had ten fewer employees and were doing over $2 million in annual revenue. So, we were doing more revenue with fewer employees. It took a lot of work, but that's when I hired a business coach.

Another big part of managing your people is understanding their perspective. One of my employees told me one time, 'You never tell me that I do a good job.' My response to him was, 'Did you get your paycheck this week?' He said he did, and I said, 'That means you're doing a good job. Because when you're not, you won't be here.' That kind of response doesn't work in today's world. As an employer, you have to realize that your employees have to come first. Your employees want your appreciation. They want recognition for their contributions. Even though you, as the owner, never get that - your employees want and need it.

I also foolishly thought the recession wasn't going to hit me. So, I was running on high liabilities, meaning I had lots of loans and high debt. I also lost a big customer, and I didn't try to keep them because I thought I'd find another one. Simultaneously, as the recession was starting to hit, we had a massive number of competitors come into the market. Plus, consumers stopped using restoration companies. I was faced with a moment where I was looking at going out of business.

The other big one is the day I had to tell my employees that I sold the [UltraClean] business. I had to go through that nine-month transaction without being able to tell them. It was emotionally draining. You go to work every day, and you almost feel like you're lying to them. But at the same time, you have to. You can't tell an employee because if the word gets out, you break confidentiality. Then you could lose the deal.

With Dillon Plumbing, I bought the business on a Thursday afternoon. Friday morning, when the old owner introduced me as the new owner, I lost half the company. Two employees quit, and I decided not to hire another one. Within 12 hours, I lost more than half the employees. The difference with Dillon plumbing was that I recognized something could happen, and I was planning for it."

How did you survive the recession with UltraClean and come back? You were able to turn things around. Can you tell me about that process and how you got there?

"The first thing I did was cut all unnecessary spending. That's number one. You have to identify every expense you have. You need to know where you are financially at any given moment. What that means is sometimes payables don't get entered, or you have a job with expenses out there that hasn't come in yet. So, you have to have an immediate perfect picture of your financial situation. That was number one.

The second thing is you have to downsize. Unfortunately, that means cutting people. You have to figure out how you can operate with half as many people. At the same time, while fear is going through the company, I had to reestablish confidence that we're going to make it through this. Even though you yourself worry that you may not be able to make it. Because if your people are worried about whether the company will survive or not, you're going to lose them. They're going to look for another, more secure job. That was a big deal. I was scared as hell on the inside, trying to establish confidence for them to stay. It didn't necessarily work because some people quit and found other jobs, and people naturally weed themselves out. But, that's one less person that you have to let go if things go downhill.

On a personal note, you have to live lean. We had to remove all debt. We sold all our vehicles that had loans on them. We bought older vehicles or kept our older vehicles that we didn't have any loans on. We cut every expense that we could except for cable, which was the internet and the phones. There were two leases. I had a phone lease and a copier lease that I could not break.

That being said, I'll never do a lease again because leases cannot be broken. Unfortunately, I had two copiers on lease. One of them was not being used, but I was still paying for it every month. If you're having financial trouble, communicate with your vendors. If you don't communicate with them, they're going to send you to collections. If you want to stay out of collections, give your vendors an idea of where you are financially. That was probably the biggest reason that we survived. I told my landlord my situation, and then he let me go six months without paying rent. My landlord had a reputation for being a hard ass, but he took a chance on me because I was open and honest with him. If you can't pay a bill, you have to be honest. And that's a hard conversation to have. Communication is crucial with people that you owe money to.

At home, we sold everything that we did not need to accumulate cash. I remember my wife bringing a recliner back to Costco. She exchanged the recliner for food. We used Craigslist to sell tons of hunting stuff and all my personal hobby stuff. It was bittersweet. It felt uplifting to have some cash and get rid of stuff, but it was also sad. I haven't gone duck hunting since, and I used to go all the time.

You also need to go to counseling, and my counselor allowed me to come in at times without payment. That was a big deal because you have to talk about the hell that you're going through. Counseling helps business owners because just getting the stuff out that you don't have anybody else to talk to relieves you mentally. At least for that one hour when you're with them."

About how long did it take you to turn things around at UltraClean?

"It took about five years. We got out of the construction side of the business, and just focused on the cleaning and restoration. I let my whole construction crew go. We still performed the services, but we outsourced to contractors. This was creative at the time. Nobody was doing it. I found a contractor who was affected by the recession. He knew my work and agreed to work together. He carried the cost and would collect the money. When he got paid, he gave me a 10% percent referral fee. That 10% of profit had no cost associated with, so I put it directly towards debt. That 10% went a long way. That helped the company survive, and it's thriving today.

The other side of it is you have to do the work of three or four people. Unfortunately, that means 20-hour days, seven days a week. It's mentally and physically exhausting, but you have to do what you have to do. My wife and kids would come out and do demolitions with me. With every job, you have to look at how you can make it as profitable as possible. In years four and five, we went from 26 people to 16 people. Then we went to 10 people. In 2012, we were down to three people doing the work of six. My staff put in the hours just like I did. They are amazing people.

Really, it boils down to you need to watch every penny. You have to examine whether your services are profitable or not. If you're not making a profit on it, then don't do it."

How did being an entrepreneur affect your personal life?

"There are days that I recognize doing something else would be much more comfortable. I mean, being an entrepreneur is a hard road to take. At the same time, I think of the gifts that I have been given. I get to teach my kids business skills and work ethic. I can give them experiences that I wouldn't have been able to if I worked for somebody else. We travel a lot. We go out to eat. We live comfortably. I believe all those luxuries would be limited if I were an employee.

It all comes down to fulfillment. Being an entrepreneur suits my nature because I want to have competition in my life. I want to feel like I'm winning. Running a business and owning a business is a game. If I can succeed at that, it's an everyday challenge. When you own a business, you have to condition your mind, body, everything else to be successful. You can win one day, but you may lose the next. Every day is a new race. An athlete trains and conditions for a race. They can win a medal, and that's the end. With a business, you might win today, but tomorrow will bring a whole new set of challenges. That right there feeds your heart. It creates a fire in your spirit. I believe business owners live on hope because they always hope for one thing or another, but we never achieve it.

I think of the personal growth I've had as a leader. Being a successful business owner has forced me to be a better husband and father because all those traits apply in business, just like they do at home. If I do well as a business owner, I do well as a father. I reap the rewards of both."

How do you handle negativity or naysayers in your life or in your business?

"I've had friends who have been way more financially successful than me. Yet, I've had to cut them out of my life because their negativity, egotism, and arrogance has had a negative impact on me. When you look at the negativity in the world, like looking at politics or religion, we all have different beliefs. And that's fine. You have to learn how to ignore the noise. But you can't let criticism that comes from an employee or a customer impact how you feel about yourself. If someone doesn't like what you've done or the decisions you've made, you can't allow that to make you think differently about yourself.

Business owners must have confidence. You have to be confident that you can do what is that you're supposed to do. You have to feel comfortable with yourself, because if you're worried about what everybody else thinks about you, your mind will not be focused on what it should be focused on. At the same time, you have to be able to take criticism. You have to be able to decipher whether or not there's something for you to learn. And if there's not, you have to be able to disagree with the criticism and move on.

That's a significant trait that's helped me over the years. I do not allow things to impact me. If they impact me, it's only momentarily because I can't go to bed with something on my mind. If we're critical of ourselves, that means we're going to be critical of others - which could be our spouse, children, or employees. And criticism never leads to anything positive in the workplace or at home.

You have to be tough and allow things to roll off your back. You have to pick and choose your battles and have a clear understanding of what your values are. If someone is trying to get you to compromise your values, you have to stick up for them. If someone has a problem with something that's not a high value of mine, I don't care. Pick and choose your battles, and always take a moment to think before you respond.

There's no question that people have had opinions about me. From the many events I've done, I hear a lot of criticism. I remember one piece of criticism in particular. It was quoted once in the Idaho Business Review about worker's comp or taxes. Someone said something like, 'He probably just works his employees to death.' It was one of those comments that you just have to shrug it off."

What keeps you going through the more challenging times?

"My 'why' for doing what I do is what keeps me going in the end. In the beginning, with UltraClean, it was all about making money and living a particular lifestyle. My mentality changed at the end of my UltraClean career. Now, what I choose to work for at Dillon is making a positive impact personally and financially in my employees' lives. My time with UltraClean was focused a lot about building a name for myself. That turned into something different at Dillon. I now want to make a positive impact as an employer.

Tied up with that is trying to figure out to change and improve an industry. With UltraClean, I created a business model that was unlike any other restoration company, which is why I eventually sold the business for what I did. With Dillon Plumbing, also I'm looking for ways to change the industry. I don't quite have that defined yet. One thing I know I can change now is creating the best place to work, where employees can see themselves just as I see myself - as an essential part of this business."

Looking back, is there anything that you would have done differently?

"Sure. Looking back on selling the business, I would have prepared better. Three years before selling it, I would have set myself up differently for tax strategies. I would have lived my life leaner before I sold the business instead of learning how to do it after selling it. What that means is you get used to having a check come every week. You cut that check off, but you're still accustomed to spending money really quickly. That'd be a book that I could write: *How to Blow a Million Dollars in a Year*."

What's one piece of advice you'd give to somebody thinking about starting their own business?

"I'd suggest buying a business instead of starting a business. With UltraClean, it took me 15 years before people hired UltraClean with no idea of why they called us specifically and not one of the other restoration companies in the area. To me, that means that we'd finally become a household name in our community. People hired us, and they didn't know why, but they knew of us. It wasn't because they knew me or somebody else within the company. They just thought we were established professionals. What I had to go through in that 15 years was not easy. But, I learned lots of lessons along the way.

Buy a business, but that doesn't mean it has to be a successful business. There are so many people who start-up businesses that they just want to get out of, so you can take them over for almost nothing. There are lots of ways to get into business. You could assume a business. Assuming something that's already established gets you that much further ahead than when you start a business from nothing."

What about somebody facing burnout, struggling with revenue, and at that point where they get overwhelmed and are thinking about throwing in the towel. What would you tell that person?

"It depends on where they're at in their business. If someone has a successful business and they're burned out, I would tell them to look at selling the business. Because I was there, and selling my business was a long transaction. I looked at three years out. I knew I needed three years of increased profitability before I could sell my business. It's not when I was planning on selling my business, but I knew that I needed three positive years of increased revenue and profit. That gave me a goal and motivated me when I lacked motivation before.

Planning for selling your business is like creating a goal or roadmap for where you want to go. If you can get to the place where your business has is sellable, you can either sell it or keep it. But at least you have that option. 95% of businesses are not sellable. If you want to be that 5%, you have to do certain things. It takes years to get there. But planning for it creates a challenge for business owners who are tired of the mundane day-to-day operations. It gives you something new to focus on.

The other side is that if your business is struggling and you're not able to make it, the first thing you need to do is stop and ask for help. You have to figure out who the right person is to help you. There are business coaches and mentors out there that I found did not fit me or my style. And it has cost me money and time to figure that out. It's not that they're not good - they just didn't fit me. That's number one. You need help and guidance to get yourself out of the situation you're in. You need someone to hold you accountable, motivate you, and listen to your deepest, darkest secrets. You need to get an outside perspective.

The second part of that is you have to realize everything you've done to get yourself to that point will not work and change your outcome. You need to think, 'I'm doing things like everybody else. Now how do I create something unique?' Only niche businesses survive. That's all built around your thoughts and beliefs, which become your business model."

.

18 STRATEGY SESSION: ALWAYS BE LEARNING

When my husband transitioned from Army paratrooper to Army recruiter, I gave him a crash course in the world of sales. This, of course, was not complete without a *Glengarry Glen Ross* watch party. The film is a harsh look at the world of hard sales and the brutal nature of cold calling – and remains one of my favorites. Alec Baldwin has one scene in the movie and delivers one of the most iconic lines in the film: "Always Be Closing."

While sales are vital to the success of a business – it's not the defining attribute of a successful entrepreneur. Anyone can close a deal (well, almost anyone), but not everyone can scale a company. So, what's the difference? The difference is the ability and the discipline to maintain a student mentality throughout the life of your business. It's true that you cannot know everything there is to know about running a business, but the more you can grow your knowledge and experience – the more effective you will be. Instead of focusing on "Always Be Closing," shift your focus to "Always be Learning."

I asked Brandon to sit for an interview because of the balance he found between growing a business and growing his own knowledge base as an entrepreneur. In fact, it became a cornerstone of his business model. While Brandon was building UltraClean, he also branched out. He hosted his radio show and podcast – Wright Stuff Radio - that featured local and national entrepreneurial personalities, each with a different topic and insight for business success. On a local level, Brandon created a unique networking function called the SmokeOut, where he would invite the local business community, host an educational speaker, and feed his guests smoked tri-tip with all the trimmings. It was one of the consistently highest attended networking events in the community. It had nothing to do with UltraClean –

but everyone knew Brandon, and the business grew from that. The focus on both of these projects was educating the local business community – and himself.

Building a Culture of Learning in Your Business

When we talk about business growth, we're not only referring to employee count or revenue. We are also talking about the growth of knowledge and experience. Remaining stagnant in your education is a death sentence for an entrepreneur. I'm not just referring to academic endeavors – but also learning from your peers and experts in your industry. The fact that you are reading this book right now tells me that you're already invested in this effort on some level – and I applaud you for that. What can you do to build a lifestyle of learning for yourself and a growth culture for your business? Let's start by breaking things down into foundational categories needed for small business success and building a lifelong learning plan.

Sales and Marketing Training

A business cannot sustain itself without revenue (sales), and there is no facet of business that changes faster than marketing best practices. Therefore, it makes sense that sales and marketing education is at the forefront of your educational goals. After all, you'll likely spend your entire career learning new things in this field. I should know, I've been a marketing professional for nearly two decades, and I'm still learning something new about my field all the time.

So, how do you approach continuing education in the field of marketing and sales? The best place to start is to go back to chapter six of this book and tap into your existing customer relationships. One of the best ways to learn how to market your business effectively is to ask the consumer what they need from you to make the purchase. Where do they prefer to take in information? What do they need to trust you? The best experts in the field cannot answer those questions better than your unique customers – and your customers are a lot cheaper to talk to. Connecting with this audience, taking notes, and testing new options is a great way to grow your marketing and sales practice.

There will be certain areas that your customers cannot teach you – specifically, the use and practical application of technology in your marketing efforts. Your customers may prefer to consume information on social media, but if you don't know how to get that content to them using the platform of choice – you won't be successful. When you want to grow your technical skill as it relates to marketing and sales, I recommend starting with the platforms themselves. All major online marketing platforms offer virtual classes and certifications on current best practices for their tools. Most importantly, they keep these courses current.

One of the biggest mistakes I find in entrepreneurs and marketers looking to improve their practice is falling down the black hole of YouTube self-help marketing videos. There is a lot of information out there, and – like much of the marketing industry – there is a lot of snake oil. I do not allow my employees to use YouTube resources when working with clients or building their training – because the quality of information is wildly varied in quality. As an entrepreneur, your time is money, so why would you waste it on outdated or inaccurate information? Start with the platform certifications so you can speak intelligently with industry professionals when you need to build that skillset or outsource marketing and sales tasks.

When it comes to sales training – good, old-fashioned experience is an excellent training tool. I also recommend a book by one of my colleagues, Scott Marker, called *Let's Get It On! Realistic Strategies For Winning The Sales Game* for practical sales tips. *The Win Without Pitching Manifesto* by Blair Enns is also a favorite in my entrepreneurial library. You can find both on Amazon and the First Dollar Feeling website on the Resources page, along with the platform certifications previously discussed to get you started on your sales and marketing training journey.

Operations and Logistics Training

As you bring in new customers, you need to manage them, your team, and your supply chain. Then, there are all of the other administrative aspects of running a business. Regardless of your industry, there is a lot of work that goes on behind the scenes of any successful business. That's where operations and logistics come into play. Without a firm grasp of best practices in this area, even the best marketing strategy will fail because you won't be able to deliver on your commitments.

This is an area where traditional collegiate education can come in handy. Your local community college likely has a two-year business management program, where many aspects of business operations will be covered. Many colleges also offer courses or certifications in logistics and supply chain operations if you are moving products rather than services. You don't need to earn a full degree, but cementing your understanding of the necessary foundational skills will help your business sustainability. If you've been in business for several years and you're still struggling – there may be a crack in that knowledge foundation. To fix a problem, you have to know how to identify it first.

If this is not an attractive option for you, you can also visit the Small Business Administration (SBA). Local and national SBA offices typically offer workshops or online classes in different areas of operations and logistics. These classes are also a great way of finding a mentor through the SBA and its affiliated programs. Start by visiting the SBA website to see what's available in your area.

Mentors and industry experts are other excellent resources for operations and logistics training for both you and your team. I have recommended joining your industry association previously in this book – and this is another benefit of being a member. Most industry associations hold conferences, certifications, webinars, and similar activities to help you succeed in business. It can be an excellent resource for building your understanding of various aspects of your business.

Finally, participating in community networking events – like Brandon's "SmokeOut" event is a great way to meet new people while getting tips for running your business. These little bite-sized functions may not allow you to do a deep dive into a topic, but it can open your eyes to new ideas you want to explore. Then, you can find more in-depth training on the things that apply. Best of all, you get to build your network at the same time. If nothing else, I've found that attending these events helps keep me in the right mindset of growth as an entrepreneur – and that's important for resiliency as you tackle your own business.

Employee Retention and Management

If your business grows sustainably, you cannot be the only one holding all of the answers. You need team members who have the knowledge and experience to take things off of your plate. Otherwise, you – the business owner – are working twenty-four hours a day, seven days a week. Nobody goes into business to do that. So, you have to invest in the growth and education of your staff. Not only does it help you get competent support, but it also fosters loyalty from your staff – thereby reducing high turnover costs.

Your employees will be looking to you first to buy into this idea of being a lifelong learner as a key to success. Start by setting the example and providing opportunities for them to participate. In my business, I tell my employees to note any areas they want to explore as they go through training in the business. Then, I find opportunities for them to grow in that area. That may be sponsoring them at a conference or assisting on a project outside of their current comfort zone. For small businesses, you cannot always compete for top talent in the area of salary – but you can compete with one-on-one attention and a personal focus on their growth. The right employee will notice, and they will bring more to their role in the long run.

Crisis Adaptation Training

The Great Depression, the impact of 9/11, the 2008 recession, and the entire year of 2020. Small businesses feel the effects of crisis events unfolding on both global and local stages. Worst of all, we have very little control over what happens – we only have real control over how we respond to it. When a crisis occurs, you have very little time to build a plan and assure your team and clientele. The best way to prepare is to work through some crisis management training when things are going well to help you objectively create contingency plans for your business. Consider it an insurance policy against the roller coaster of the economy.

First - one of the biggest pitfalls for businesses in a crisis is poor communication. You can have the most well-thought-out plan to mitigate risk – but if you cannot communicate with your employees, shareholders, and customers for nothing, that plan is nearly worthless in a panicked situation. Again, this is an area where you can find resources at your local college. Many schools with a business program hold crisis communications classes. I highly recommend these courses for any entrepreneur.

Crisis adaptation is a challenging skill to learn in other areas because most crises typically stem from unexpected or unexplored concerns. How can you prepare for something you know nothing about? The truth is that you can't – not entirely anyway. However, you can build the soft skills needed to be effective in a crisis. Soft skills refer to the business's non-technical side – like emotional intelligence, communication skills, adaptability, time management, leadership, and work ethic. In truth, you can only learn so much about these in a classroom setting. Most of these skills are learned and developed in the field.

The reality is every person has these mental muscles. Just like any other muscle group, to become strong – you have to exercise. Mentors and coaches are useful resources to help you develop these skills – or at least to push you into situations where you need to use those skills. You have to be willing to be out of your comfort zone as much as possible to grow in these areas. If you don't have a mentor, consider writing down twelve activities that scare you. Then, tackle one a month for a year to help you stretch your out-of-the-box skills and intuition. These do not have to be business-related. You need to develop your resiliency and adaptability to instill those skills in your team. So, start by tackling big things that scare you. The more you do this, the less tentative you'll be when faced with an unexpected obstacle.

The Importance of the Educator Role as an Entrepreneur

As you build all of this knowledge and experience, you are missing an opportunity if you do not give it away. To be a successful entrepreneur in today's world, you need to make your mark as a thought leader. That may be on a local level, national level, or international level. Regardless of your goals, when you open a business, people look to you as a leader. You can make millions in revenue, but you are not a leader unless you bring other people along with you. The best way to do this is to share your knowledge and experience. Consider: What do you want your legacy to be? Build your business culture accordingly.

Learn, Then Do.

Of course, all of the world's education and experience won't do you a bit of good if you don't apply it to your sales and operations strategies. If you're spending the time investing in your education and that of your team – find new ways to put those skills to work. Remember, the ultimate goal is growth. Growth does not occur if you do not tie your new knowledge into something that will help you build revenue and keep your clients happy.

After all, we must never forget – *"coffee is for closers."*

KEY TAKEAWAYS

KEY TAKEAWAYS

KEY TAKEAWAYS

19 IF AT FIRST YOU DON'T SUCCEED

It seems we've almost come to the end of our journey together, at least for now. My goal with the First Dollar Feeling project is to help business owners find strength, joy, and sustainability in their business. I believe wholeheartedly in the concept of entrepreneurs helping entrepreneurs. So how can I help you prepare to best apply what you've learned from fellow entrepreneurs in your business? Let's take a moment to review the pillars of entrepreneurial success to help you do a temperature check on your own business.

The Pillars of Business Success

If you Google "pillars of business success," you're going to find hundreds of articles all widely differing from any sort of agreement about what it takes to be successful in business. However, after pouring over the interviews in this book, talking to the more than 200 business owners I've worked with over the last 16 years, and reflecting upon my college education, work as a business mentor, and time as an employer– I have found that all of the business advice out there boils down to five core components. I want you to use these as cornerstones to check the status of your business objectively.

People

People are important. Relationships are important. In fact, you cannot build upon the other 'pillars of success' without people. Throughout this book, we've talked about the different relationships you need in business.

From customers to referral partners, and mentors to employees – you cannot grow your business without people's loyalty.

Consider your business. Review the following items, and make your notes in the pages after this chapter. If you find something that you do not know, ask someone in your business who would know the answer. Be open to accepting things that you may not want to hear. Our goal here is growth – and that endeavor is never comfortable.

Do you have employees? If so, what is the average length of tenure for an employee in your business? When was the last time you checked in with them on an individual basis? How do you monitor the satisfaction of your employees? Do your employees demonstrate competency and quality in their work? How would you describe the energy in your team? How would your newest employee describe the energy of your team?

How do you stay connected to your customers? Have your sales increased or decreased overall in the last three years? Do you have an influx of new customers? How has that number changed over the last 24 months? How has that number changed over the last 12 months? How many online reviews do you have? What is your star rating? How many online reviews do your top five competitors have? What are their star ratings?

Finally, who are your top ten referral sources? How frequently do you connect with them? How much business have you sent them in the course of the relationship? Are the referrals you get from these sources quality, or are they deal-seekers? How active are these referral sources in networks that matter to your business?

Once you've answered these questions, you may find a few concerns that immediately jump out at you. If you're struggling in your business – you now have a clear problem that you can address right now. Make a note, make a plan, and start work on correcting the problem. Engage your team, get a mentor for this issue, take a course from your local Small Business Administration (SBA), or find a book or a podcast that deals with this problem – you will find a library of resources and recommendations on the First Dollar Feeling website.

Cash

People are essential, but you cannot maintain your business without proper cash flow. It's the number one killer of small businesses, according to the SBA. You need the money to keep the proverbial doors of your business open, to pay your employees, to continue to create your product or provide your service, and to generally keep food on the table. I strongly recommend engaging an accountant to review your existing cash flow budget. If you do not have access to an accountant, you can run the budget yourself to get a good understanding of where you are. You'll need the data on your bank statements, accounts receivable, inventory, accounts payable, and credit terms. You'll also want to pull your sales reports for the last two years – to provide a side-by-side comparison of growth or decline. There is a free cash flow budgeting tool with detailed instructions on the First Dollar Feeling website. Gather your data, download the tool, and run your budget.

This exercise will force you to see issues with your cash flow that may be prohibiting business growth. You'll need to objectively review your spending and make cuts as needed. Unless you have substantial accounting experience, if you do not have an accountant to review this information with you – I would begin working towards hiring one as soon as possible. You need someone who can keep you in financial check.

Vision

We've talked about marketing, employee management, differentiators, and helping yourself stand out from the crowd in business. That all comes from your entrepreneurial vision. If you do not know where your business is going – what your purpose is – you'll never get there. At least not without wasting a lot of time and money. Without a clear mission, you'll never foster loyalty from your customers, referral partners, or employees.

Can you explain the purpose of your business in two sentences or less? If your answer is no, you have some work to do. Walk yourself through the process of writing a business plan. If you already have a business plan and you still cannot answer that question – go back and read chapter eight of this book. Then, write another business plan. There is a simple to use, free business plan template on the First Dollar Feeling website to guide you through the process.

Process

Once your vision is clear, you need the processes in place to keep your business operating as efficiently as possible. This affects your customer satisfaction, cash flow, employee engagement, and ability to weather a crisis. Review the processes in your business.

Do you have defined and documented operating procedures for your marketing, customer service, accounting, and logistics departments in your business? Are there areas in your business that could be automated for efficiency? Are the processes you have in place contributing to issues with customers? Are the processes you have in place contributing to issues with your employees? Are there areas that could be streamlined or removed to use fewer resources?

The sooner you define these processes, the easier it will be for you to build revenue, increase customer buy-in, and onboard new employees with lower turnover. Finding the balance between automation and outsourcing tasks associated with each process becomes a much more palatable endeavor when you have mapped out what you need to happen to accomplish your mission. Review chapter ten of this book again if you need insight into identifying areas to improve efficiency.

Adaptability

This book was published in 2020, the year we all wanted to pitch the word "unprecedented" out of a moving car window. Everything, every day, presented some new issue that required change. For the first time in a long time, that was felt worldwide. Nearly every business owner in America found themselves in a very similarly battered boat. I wish there were a template I could give you to prove or improve your adaptability and your business to guard against such things. That template does not exist. In the last chapter, I discussed the importance of soft skills for entrepreneurs. Even if you are in the thick of the battle, I'd advise taking steps to develop those skills. You will need them for the road ahead, and now is as good a time as any to get started.

I'd also like to reinforce the importance of finding a mentor in your struggles. It is so incredibly challenging to pull yourself out of the moment when you are drowning. An objective third party will help you visualize a path forward if that's what you choose to do. In chapter sixteen of this book, I detailed various ways to find a mentor to suit your needs. If you still find yourself struggling with this, visit the First Dollar Feeling website to connect with a member of our team. We have a network of individuals and organizations whose sole purpose is to keep small businesses strong and sustainable. We'll help you find the right fit.

What to Do When It's Not Working

On the back cover, the words "what do you do when the passion dies?" are in bold type. So, what do you do? What happens when your best efforts just don't pan out? What happens when you want to quit? The answer is simple, like all the best solutions are.

If you are struggling – you ask for help.

Success in business is not something anybody can do on their own. Entrepreneurship is not a solo act. If you are overwhelmed, I hope that this book injected valuable insight into the dark clouds forming in your business. Every company is different. Your needs are going to vary from any other entrepreneur. There is no magic paragraph I could write to solve every issue for every business owner. You need to seek out individual support to help you address the most caustic issues in your business. Fortunately, this support is relatively accessible.

I invite you to utilize the library of free resources and templates on the First Dollar Feeling website. They were created to help entrepreneurs like you find their way back to joy in their businesses. You can also visit your Small Business Administration, Small Business Development Center, or local SCORE office for individual support. You can also engage with your local Chamber of Commerce to find additional resources that may be available in your community. Finally, if you need to be connected to support and don't know where to turn, I invite you to reach out to the First Dollar Feeling team on social media, and we will help guide you to the right resources for your needs.

If you have a vision and your business isn't serving that purpose – don't be afraid to make a change. To be an entrepreneur is to be an innovator – to see the world differently and to make it better by what you do. Something along the line put an idea in your head and made you crazy enough to open a business. You need to find a way to get back to that original dream. Reach out to your fellow business owners and the communities we've built around us. We're all still here with you, working for that first dollar feeling.

To keeping the faith.

KEY TAKEAWAYS

KEY TAKEAWAYS

KEY TAKEAWAYS

ABOUT THE AUTHOR

Erika Heeren is an award-winning digital marketing and public relations professional with more than 16 years of experience spanning multiple industries and more than 200 clients. With a long-standing passion for guerrilla marketing tactics, she also works with small businesses and non-profit organizations to provide affordable, professional-quality content development and outreach services. Her clients include local small business owners, marketing agencies, public universities, media outlets, authors, IT firms, and non-profit organizations.

As President of The Small Business Marketing Studio, Heeren works to connect qualified military-affiliated professionals with small businesses in need of support. She also has a career coaching program designed to help military spouses, first responder spouses, and transitioning veterans find sustainable careers in marketing and communications. As a consultant and contract CMO, Heeren provides corporate training and project management services for enterprise and small businesses looking to improve their internal and external communications strategy.

Erika Heeren is an experienced and engaging speaker in the areas of women's issues, small business development, digital marketing, and the issues facing veterans and the military family community. She is also an outspoken advocate for veteran and military spouse employment, education, and entrepreneurship. She also frequently writes for various print and web publications on small business development and military family advocacy topics.

Heeren is a military spouse – her husband, Jacob, is currently an active duty soldier in the United States Army. They are currently stationed in the mid-Atlantic region, where SSG Heeren serves as a recruiter. Erika has two children (Ben and Lottie), two dogs (Piper and Penelope), and one obstinate cat (Bernie Boots). She enjoys reading, writing, and playing the piano in her spare time.

Heeren is a 2019 Idaho Business Review Women of the Year honoree, a 2019 Women in Content Marketing Awards – Mentorship winner, a 2016 Idaho Press Awards recipient, a Suburban Newspapers of America Design Award recipient, and has been featured on Inc.com as one of the Top 10 Women in Content Marketing in 2019.

BIBLIOGRAPHY

"2016 ASE Tables: Characteristics of Business," U.S. Census Bureau. accessed November 2020, https://www.census.gov/programs-surveys/ase/data/tables.html

"2018 Military Family Lifestyle Survey Comprehensive Report." Blue Star Families. Accessed November 2020. https://bluestarfam.org/wp-content/uploads/2019/03/2018MFLS-ComprehensiveReport-DIGITAL-FINAL.pdf

"2019 Retention Report," The Work Institute, accessed November 2020, https://info.workinstitute.com/hubfs/2019%20Retention%20Report/Work%20Institute%202019%20Retention%20Report%20final-1.pdf

"Ambition and gender at work," *The Institute of Leadership & Management*, accessed November 2020. https://www.institutelm.com/resourceLibrary/ambition-and-gender-at-work.html

"Americans Prefer to Buy from Socially Conscious Companies This Holiday Shopping Season, SAP Study Finds," PRNewsWire, December 04, 2018, https://www.prnewswire.com/news-releases/americans-prefer-to-buy-from-socially-conscious-companies-this-holiday-shopping-season-sap-study-finds/

Bryant, Adam. "Good C.E.O.'s are insecure (and know it)." *The New York Times*. October 9, 2010. https://www.nytimes.com/2010/10/10/business/10corner.html?_r=1

Gallo, Amy. "The Value of Keeping the Right Customers," *The Harvard Business Review*, October 29 2014. https://hbr.org/2014/10/the-value-of-keeping-the-right-customers

Giang, Vivian. "8 female leaders on how to overcome what's holding women back." *Fast Company*. September 10, 2014. https://www.fastcompany.com/3035478/8-successful-women-leaders-on-how-to-overcome-whats-holding-women-back

Haider, Anser & Rasay, Stefen. "Zoom's massive growth amid COVID-19 set to continue after pandemic, analysts say," *S&P Global Market Intelligence*,

June 4, 2020.
https://www.spglobal.com/marketintelligence/en/news-insights/latest-news-headlines/zoom-s-massive-growth-amid-covid-19-set-to-continue-after-pandemic-analysts-say-58907516

Hannon, Kerry. "The number one way women can succeed more at work." *Forbes*. April 24, 2014.
https://www.forbes.com/sites/nextavenue/2014/04/24/the-no-1-way-women-can-succeed-more-at-work/?sh=2d7659ccb17c

"How Zoom became so popular during social distancing," CNBC, accessed November 2020,
https://www.cnbc.com/2020/04/03/how-zoom-rose-to-the-top-during-the-coronavirus-pandemic.html

Langford, Joe; Clance, Pauline Rose (Fall 1993). "The impostor phenomenon: recent research findings regarding dynamics, personality and family patterns and their implications for treatment". *Psychotherapy: Theory, Research, Practice, Training*. 30 (3): 495–501.

Locke, Taylor. "Why Barbara Corcoran 'felt like an absolute fraud' after selling her business for $66 million." *CNBC*. February 27, 2020.
https://www.cnbc.com/2020/02/27/why-barbara-corcoran-felt-like-a-fraud-after-selling-her-business.html#:~:text=Despite%20building%20a%20multi%2Dmillion,of%20her%20accomplishments%2C%20she%20says.

"Military Family Programming Survey 2019 Results." Military Family Advisory Network. Accessed November 2020.
https://militaryfamilyadvisorynetwork.org/wpcontent/uploads/MFAN2019SurveyResults.pdf

Warrell, Margie. "Afraid of being 'found out?' How to overcome impostor syndrome. *Forbes*. April 3, 2014.
https://www.forbes.com/sites/margiewarrell/2014/04/03/impostor-syndrome/?sh=7c08343748a9

Zimmerman, Ben. "How adapting to consumer trends can safeguard small businesses," *Forbes*, August 3 2020.
https://www.forbes.com/sites/forbesbusinesscouncil/2020/08/03/how-adapting-to-consumer-trends-can-safeguard-small-businesses/?sh=2e4ec0c95f74

Love the book? Leave a review on Amazon.com!